What's On Your Fork?!

EASY, HEALTHY MEALS FOR EVERYBODY

What's On Your Fork?!: Easy, healthy recipes for everybody
Written by Shelley Loving

Published by Loving Life Publications
Van Alstyne, Texas
USA

www.shelleycanhelp.com

Contact publisher for bulk orders and permission requests.

Copyright © 2022 by Shelley Loving

Cover and interior book design & formatting by
Leesa Ellis of 3 ferns books ►— **www.3fernsbooks.com**

Photography by Shelley Loving

Printed in the United States of America.

Library of Congress Control Number: 2022914830

ISBN (Hardback): 979-8-218-04071-0

What's On Your Fork?!

EASY, HEALTHY MEALS FOR EVERYBODY

Shelley Loving INHC, CNE, CPC

Loving Life
PUBLICATIONS

Foreword

Having grown up in the same small town as her, I knew Shelley's parents and grandparents. However, I didn't know Shelley personally until about three years ago. That was when I discovered that she not only loved her job, but she loved sharing good news about food with everyone. How appropriate is it that Shelley's last name is Loving? I promise, she did not make that up! Loving is what she does!

I have always enjoyed cooking and thought I knew just about all there was to placing a meal on the table right up until my doctor told me that my cholesterol was past the danger zone and headed into the upper reaches of the stratosphere. Since I didn't want to take medication for the problem, I decided to try changing my condition through diet. But, where to start? How could I bring about change for me while still providing tasty meals for the family? Several mutual friends told me that Shelley Loving was the answer to my dilemma.

I contacted Shelley and she jumped right into action. She provided menus with recipes that I could easily make with ingredients that were readily available. The best part was that my family also enjoyed my "new" meals. Within one month, my cholesterol lowered over one hundred points. ONE HUNDRED POINTS! I can honestly proclaim that Shelley lovingly saved my life!

I am so excited about this cookbook. I know that Shelley has placed her "Loving" stamp of approval on each ingredient and process. I promise you that this cookbook will educate you about ingredients and open your eyes to a new approach to meals. I am living proof that it is never too late to learn new tips and improve your overall health.

ENJOY!

Diana Smith

Introduction

Healthier cooking definitely hasn't been a lifelong habit of mine. It's one that took a life-threatening health scare to really "shake" me and wake me up to the importance of my food choices.

In 2014, my forty-one-year-old husband had a massive heart attack. He had one hundred percent blockage in his left circumflex artery. They call that artery the widow maker and I still count my blessings that this heart attack didn't make me a widow. I wasn't ready. I had just married my best friend and I wasn't even close to being able to handle losing him.

As the cardiologist was making his last room visit before our hospital departure, he told Neil that he would be on six or seven medications for the rest of his life. We both looked at each other, shook our heads no, and said, "Oh no he won't."

I'll never forget the moment we arrived home from the hospital and Neil laid down. I hopped onto the bed and as I put my head on his chest, I could hear his heart beating. That was when I lost it. I did the uncontrollable sob; you know...the ugly cry. I mean I had held it together for three solid days. I was the strong one. I had to be strong for Neil. But once he was home and away from the hospital, he held me tight, and I wept. My tears soaked his shirt. I hated to break in front of him. Afterall, he was the patient. Just hearing the soft sounds of his steady heartbeat made our entire future flash in front of me and that was when I knew we had to change things.

I instinctively turned to food as a way to help him get better. We were determined to get him off some of these medications and we knew we needed to try a more holistic approach.

As I was searching endlessly on Google for "heart healthy recipes," I found so much contradicting information. As luck would have it...you know what? I don't believe in luck one single bit. As the stars aligned and listened to my soul in 2017, I stumbled upon the Institute for Integrative Nutrition. I was so passionate about helping Neil that I decided to attend school to learn more about holistic health and nutrition.

As I soaked in all this knowledge from IIN, I started putting these new eating habits into practice and introducing new ingredients into our meals. Over the course of a year, Neil and I saw a HUGE difference in our health and our physical appearance. The chronic inflammation we both suffered from was reduced and we both felt better than ever. Heck, I was feeling amazing, and I wasn't even the "sick" one.

My joint pain went away and so did my dull headaches. I had more clarity, and my eyes were brighter. My seasonal allergies vanished, and I slept better. All of this was happening just by switching out some ingredients and avoiding those foods that cause inflammation.

Food can cause inflammation, or it can reduce it. This was a game changer for me. Once I figured that part out, that I had so much control over how we felt and how our bodies reacted was mind-blowing. With the transformation, we were both seeing in our health and how we looked, I knew I couldn't keep this information to myself. That was where Shelley Can Help was born. In 2018, I decided to start a business helping others learn ways to cook and eat a little bit healthier. I had no idea where I was going with it or what I was going to do, but I knew I wanted to help people. This information isn't taught in school and the standard American diet DEFINITELY doesn't have our health in mind.

I loved IIN. I learned so much and yet I was yearning for more knowledge. So, in 2019, I attended the Academy of Culinary Nutrition. This school was incredible. It really taught me how to treat food like medicine. It taught me so much about the "why" behind ingredients and my recipes became intentional; yet another game-changer for me and my business.

This was where I began to create my own recipes, using real whole ingredients. I wanted to keep my recipes simple-ish so that even those that hate cooking could follow the recipe.

In 2021, I decided to go to yet another school. I wanted to hone my culinary skills, so I attended Rouxbe online culinary school where I became a certified professional cook. This gave me more confidence in my kitchen skills so that I could create more recipes using some of the culinary skills I picked up in school.

It is now 2022 and I am definitely not done with school. I love to learn, not only for me but so that I can help more people with their own healthy food journey. Watching people improve their health through food is my where my heart and soul lie. When an individual reaches out to me with an email to tell me how much I have "saved their life," I just can't describe how wonderful it feels. If I can prevent just one person from dying of a massive heart attack, then my mission has purpose. If I can help just one person get off their statins because they are eating a healthy diet, I have won.

Like my career, this cookbook has my heart fully in it and I hope you can feel the love through my recipes. They are simple to follow. They are anti-inflammatory, and they are, most importantly, delicious!

Keeping it real

In the six-plus years I have been navigating through this healthy food journey, I have never allowed myself to feel shame or guilt when I make a poor food choice. What good would that serve me? I feel like I'm hard enough on myself with career goals, future plans, body image, comparison to others, and so on. So, I vowed to never go down that self-sabotaging thought process of "Well, you ate four Oreos, so you blew it. Might as well give up."

I see this journey with food as a friendship. It's a friendship that needs some nurturing. I will always have a relationship with food. I can't survive without it. So instead of making that relationship complicated or full of dread and resentment, I have actively chosen to embrace this relationship and treat it with the utmost love and respect. I see food choices as "how will this nourish me?" instead of an "I hate broccoli," or "I can't live without cheese" mindset. I focus on what I *can* and *should* eat instead of what I can't eat.

One aspect of my business I'm passionate about is teaching others how to love food in a healthy way, not just with healthier ingredients but with healthier thoughts about the recipes they create. Food is emotional. We eat with our heart, soul, memories, hormones, and love.

Eating healthy isn't perfect. It's messy with a lot of hills and valleys, but I'm passionate about shifting your mindset on healthier cooking. I want you to have the wiggle room for uh-ohs and unhealthy moments. There can be a beautiful balance between making healthier food choices and enjoying those foods that aren't so healthy. I mean, let's be honest. There are some foods that simply make you close your eyes and sometimes let out a moan. I know I do!

So, let's keep it real. Let's enjoy the pizza at the Super Bowl party and the cheese board and wine when we gather with friends. But in the everyday routine of food choices, let's keep them full of nutrients that will help our bodies stay strong and healthy. Let's fill it with anti-inflammatory recipes that will allow our immune system to work at its highest level.

What are you eating Tuesday for lunch? What are you snacking on at 3 PM during that work meeting? What are you feeding your family after soccer practice Thursday evening? What are you drinking while running your errands? THESE, my friend, are the choices that matter. These are the food choices that are going to really set the tone for your health, your immune system, and your ability to stay strong.

My hope for this cookbook is that it will serve you as more than just a cookbook. It is a way for you to see inside my thoughts, beliefs, and teachings. Think of it as a workbook journal with anti-inflammatory recipes.

Think of my recipes as little worker bees, worker bees that are working so hard to boost your immune system, helping to lower the chronic inflammation in your body, and offering nourishment through essential vitamins and minerals. The best part is...they also taste really good!

I invite you into my thought processes in the development of each recipe so you can understand the "why" behind my recipes, the ingredients that go into them, and how they nourish your body and help keep you healthy.

Delicious food is a must since we eat with our eyes as well as our tastebuds. But I also want you to understand my recipes are intentional. There is a "why" behind each one and in this cookbook, I'm going to show you just that.

It's time for me to open the curtains to my heart and soul of these recipes. This is my first cookbook, but I promise it's the first of many. So, enjoy the journey of this book. I hope you can taste the love that went into each recipe.

If you have any questions along the way, please feel free to reach out to me! You can find me everywhere on social media under @shelleycanhelp or you can visit my website **www.shelleycanhelp.com**

Enjoy the recipes and I'll see you on the inside!

Notes To Help You Along

Before you dive in

You will notice that there are some ingredients that I use quite a bit throughout the book. These may be ingredients you are familiar with, or they may be foreign to you, but either way, please have an open mind. Below are some staples to have in your kitchen that are anti-inflammatory, full of nutrients, and will speed up your prep time.

- Quinoa
- Coconut oil
- Avocado oil
- Extra-virgin olive oil
- Coconut sugar
- Nutritional yeast
- Tamari
- Sea salt (NOT white table salt)
- Almond butter
- Fresh garlic (LOTS of garlic)
- Cashews
- Rice vinegar
- Apple cider vinegar

My recipes have two purposes.

Eliminate ingredients that cause inflammation. The three main food groups I avoid in every recipe are **dairy, gluten, and white refined sugar.** These food groups are extremely inflammatory so I eliminate them.

Increase ingredients that lower inflammation. There are foods that actually help you fight (lower) inflammation. These are foods like leafy greens, salmon, ginger, coconut oil, avocados, and so many more.

Contents

One Bowl Meals

1. Salmon Sushi Bowl
2. Chicken Stir Fry
3. Stuffed Pepper Bowl
4. Asian Noodle Bowl
5. Turkey & Veggies w/Chimichurri

Salmon Sushi Bowl

Servings: 2
Time: 30 minutes

Salmon

- 2 pieces salmon fillets
- ½ tsp sea salt
- ¼ tsp paprika
- ¼ tsp turmeric
- ¼ tsp black pepper

Pickled Carrot Ribbons

- 2 carrots (ribbons)
- ¼ cup rice vinegar (can use white vinegar)
- 3 Tbsp coconut sugar
- ⅛ tsp sea salt

Quinoa

- ½ cup quinoa (uncooked)
- ¼ cup cilantro (chopped)
- 1 tsp lime juice (about ¼ of a lime, squeezed)

Sriracha Mayonnaise

- 3 Tbsp mayonnaise
- 1 tsp sriracha
- ¼ tsp sesame oil

Eel Sauce

- ¼ cup tamari
- ¼ cup coconut sugar
- 1½ tsp Mirin (can use rice vinegar)
- 3 Tbsp white cooking wine
- 1 tsp arrowroot powder
- 1 Tbsp water

Bowl Add-ons

- ½ cucumber (sliced)
- 1 avocado (sliced)
- 1 Tbsp sesame seeds
- 2 stalks green onions (diced)

How it's made

1. This recipe has a lot going on, but I promise it's worth it! There are a lot of moving parts so it's important to be organized before you begin. You have four components: salmon, quinoa, sriracha mayo, and eel sauce.

2. First up, let's season the salmon. Rinse and pat your salmon dry. In a small bowl, mix together the salt, paprika, turmeric, and black pepper. Spread the seasoning mixture over the salmon fillets (fillets should be skin-side down). Set aside.

3. Time to pickle the carrots. Take a peeler to the carrots and just keep running it over the carrot in the same spot. This will form pretty carrot "ribbons." In a small bowl, add the rice vinegar, coconut sugar, and sea salt. Whisk it and then add your carrots. Make sure they are all submerged in the mixture. Set aside and let them rest.

4. Preheat your oven to 400°F. While it heats, let's make the quinoa. Rinse your quinoa and place it in a small saucepan with 1 cup of water. Bring to a boil and reduce to a very low setting, cover and cook for 6–8 minutes or until all the water is evaporated. Take it off the heat, remove the lid, and let it cool.

5. To make the spicy mayo, combine the mayo, sriracha, and sesame oil. I like to put this in a small Ziploc bag. Then I cut a small corner off and squeeze the sauce to make it pretty. If time doesn't permit, it can be poured over the serving bowls.

6. Let's get the eel sauce going on the stove. This will cook low and slow. We want to reduce it so it becomes thick like a balsamic glaze-like texture.

7. In a small saucepan over medium-low heat, add in the tamari, coconut sugar, mirin (or rice vinegar), and dry white wine (it can be cooking wine or regular wine). Whisk everything for about a minute. The sugar should be dissolved. Once it begins to bubble, turn the heat to very low and let it simmer, stirring every couple of minutes so it doesn't stick.

8. For the salmon, heat an oven-safe skillet on medium-high and add the avocado oil. Once hot, place your salmon fillets (skin-side down) in the oil and sear on both sides for 1 minute. Now place your skillet in the oven and cook the salmon for 6–7 minutes.

9. Once the salmon is done, the eel sauce should also be done. Take it off the heat. It will thicken up, but if it's not thick enough, you can take the arrowroot powder and water and mix them in a small bowl to create a slurry. Add a little at a time into the eel sauce until it thickens up. Then brush the eel sauce (glaze) onto the salmon.

10. Add the cilantro and lime juice to your quinoa and mix well. Now let's assemble your sushi bowls. Add your quinoa to the individual serving bowls, add in your salmon, carrots, cucumber, and avocado slices, and top with the mayo mixture, green onions, and sesame seeds. Enjoy! If you have any extra eel sauce, feel free to drizzle it over the bowl!

Protein: salmon, sesame seeds, and quinoa
Fiber: carrots
Healthy fat: avocado oil and avocado

Tips

Try to buy good quality mayonnaise. There should not be any refined oils in the mayo you purchase. I love the brands Chosen Foods & Primal Kitchen. They both use avocado oil in their mayonnaise

I use turmeric whenever I can. It's loaded with anti-inflammatory properties and because it's very yellow in color, I add it to most of my salmon dishes

Notes

_____

_____

_____

_____

_____

_____

Chicken Stir Fry

Servings: 4
Time: 25 minutes

- 1lb chicken breast (skinless, boneless, cut into cubes)
- 1 tsp sea salt
- ½ tsp black pepper
- 1 tsp sesame oil
- 1 tsp avocado oil (divided)
- ½ yellow onion (diced)
- 2 garlic cloves, minced
- 2 cups mushrooms (sliced)
- 2 carrots (sliced)
- 1 zucchini (large dice)
- 2 heads bok choy
- ½ cup tamari
- 3 Tbsp coconut sugar
- 1 Tbsp lime juice
- 1 Tbsp sesame seeds

How it's made

1. In a bowl add the sliced chicken with sesame oil and toss in a little sea salt and black pepper.

2. In a large skillet over medium-low heat, add the avocado oil. Once it's hot, add the sliced chicken and cook for 6–8 minutes or until cooked through. Remove the chicken from the pan and set it aside.

3. While the chicken cooks, cut up your bok choy. You want to separate the leaves from the stalks. Once you cut the leaves off, roughly chop them up and save them to add in at the end. Now slice the stalks (like you would celery) and set them aside.

4. In the same skillet you cooked the chicken in, add the remaining avocado and sauté the diced onion. Add a little sea salt to the onions and toss. Cook until they are translucent. Add the minced garlic and sauté for 1 minute.

5. Add in the mushrooms and sauté for 1–2 minutes. Once they start to sweat, add in the carrots and sauté for 1–2 minutes. Now add in the zucchini.

6. While the vegetables are cooking, whisk the tamari, coconut sugar, and lime juice in a small bowl. Pour the sauce into the vegetables, and give it all a good stir. Place a lid on the pan, and cook on low heat for 4 minutes.

7. Divide between serving bowls. Top with sesame seeds. Enjoy!

Protein: chicken
Fiber: bok choy, zucchini
Healthy fat: oils

Optional

Mix in some cooked quinoa for added texture and protein.

Notes

Stuffed Pepper Bowls

Servings: 4
Time: 50 minutes

- 1 cup brown rice, cooked
- 1 Tbsp avocado oil
- 1 yellow onion, diced
- 2 tsp sea salt
- 1 tsp oregano
- 2 tsp paprika
- ½ tsp red pepper flakes
- 1½ lbs extra-lean ground turkey
- 1 tsp avocado oil
- 2 red bell peppers (cut into chunks)
- 1 Tbsp nutritional yeast
- 2 garlic cloves, minced
- 1 can crushed tomatoes, drained
- 1 can diced tomatoes, drained
- 1 can white navy beans, rinsed & drained
- 4 stalks green onions, diced

How it's made

1. Cook the rice according to the package directions. (NOTE: you can also use quinoa).

2. Meanwhile, heat a large pot over medium-high heat. Add half the avocado oil to the pan. Add onions and after a minute, sprinkle in some sea salt. Mix them around and cook until the onions are translucent. Add the turkey to the pan, breaking it up with a wooden spoon as it cooks. Once it is cooked through and no longer pink, transfer the meat and onions to a plate and drain any excess drippings from the pan.

3. Add the remaining oil to the same pan. Sprinkle in the oregano, paprika, and red pepper flakes. Mix them around and cook for about 1 minute. Add the peppers and cook for 2–3 minutes. Add the browned turkey and onions back to the pot and give it a good stir.

4. Add the remaining ingredients to the turkey mixture (except the green onions) and simmer on low for 10–15 minutes. I prefer to put a lid on so everything stays super moist.

5. To serve, divide the turkey mixture and rice between bowls. Stir together and then top with green onions.

Protein: turkey (and quinoa if using)
Fiber: brown rice, bell pepper
Healthy fat: avocado oil

Notes

Asian Noodle Bowl

Servings: 2
Time: 20 minutes

- 2 cups gluten-free ramen noodles (or any gluten-free spaghetti)
- 1 Tbsp avocado oil
- 1 cup mushrooms, sliced
- ½ cup purple cabbage, chopped
- 1 carrot, shredded or diced
- ½ cup red bell pepper, diced
- ½ cup yellow bell pepper, diced
- 2 garlic cloves, minced

Sauce

- ½ cup almond butter
- 3 Tbsp tamari
- 1 Tbsp maple syrup
- 2 Tbsp sesame oil
- 2 Tbsp rice vinegar (or apple cider vinegar)
- ¼ cup warm water
- 1 tsp ginger, minced
- 2 garlic cloves, minced
- 1 Tbsp lime juice
- ½ tsp red pepper flakes

Bowl Add-ons

- ½ cup edamame (peas out of the pod)
- 2 Tbsp cilantro, chopped
- 1 egg (sliced)
- 1 tsp sesame seeds
- 2 stalks green onions, diced

How it's made

1. Boil your noodles according to package directions. I have good luck finding gluten-free ramen at Costco and some Asian markets.

2. Heat a skillet with the avocado oil and half the sesame oil on low. Sauté half the garlic for 1 minute. Add the mushrooms and let them sweat for 3 minutes.

3. Add in the cabbage, bell peppers, and carrots. Sauté until soft, still firm, but cooked through.

4. While the vegetables sauté, add the almond butter, tamari, maple syrup, sesame oil, vinegar or ACV, water, ginger, remaining garlic, lime juice, red pepper flakes into a small mixing bowl and whisk until smooth.

5. Place the noodles in a serving bowl, pour half the sauce over them, and mix to combine. Now place the veggies in the sauce and top with cilantro, edamame peas, the sliced boiled egg, and the diced green onions, Top with sesame seeds and enjoy!

Protein: sesame seeds, egg, edamame, almond butter
Fiber: cabbage, bell peppers
Healthy fat: oils, almond butter

Optional

Switch out your vegetables. Zucchini and bean sprouts are also great in this recipe. You can also add cooked shrimp or chicken for added protein.

Notes

Turkey & Veggies w/Chimichurri

Servings: 4
Time: 30 minutes

- 1 Tbsp avocado oil
- 1 yellow onion, diced
- 1lb extra-lean ground turkey
- 3 garlic cloves, minced
- 1 tsp dried thyme
- 1 tsp dried oregano
- 1 cup cherry tomatoes
- ¼ tsp sea salt
- 2 cups broccoli (cut into florets)
- 1 sweet potato, cubed
- 1 yellow bell pepper, largely diced
- 1 zucchini, cubed
- 2 Tbsp lemon juice

Chimichurri

- ½ cup fresh parsley
- ¼ cup fresh cilantro
- ½ cup yellow onion, diced
- 5 garlic cloves, minced
- ½ cup red bell pepper, diced
- 1 Tbsp dried oregano
- 1 tsp sea salt
- ¾ tsp red wine vinegar (can also use lemon juice)
- ¼ cup extra-virgin olive oil

Bowl Add-ons

- 2 Tbsp hemp seeds

How it's made

1. Heat avocado oil in a large skillet on low heat. Add the chopped onion and cook until translucent. Add the ground turkey and turn the heat to medium.

2. When the turkey is about half cooked, mix in the nutritional yeast. Cook until no longer pink and remove from the pan and set aside.

3. Turn heat to medium-low and in the same pan, add more avocado oil. Add the minced garlic, thyme, oregano, tomatoes, and a little sea salt. Cover and let the tomatoes cook for 5 minutes.

4. Add in the sweet potato, broccoli, and bell pepper. Stir and cover. Let cook for 5 minutes.

5. While the vegetables cook, make the chimichurri by putting the parsley, cilantro, garlic, oregano, onions, red bell pepper, red wine vinegar, and sea salt into a food processor or blender. Give everything a rough blend and slowly add in the extra virgin olive oil until everything is well blended and chopped.

6. Once the vegetables are cooked al dente, add the turkey back in and stir everything. Let everything heat up for 1–2 minutes. Add sea salt if needed.

7. Place mixture into serving bowls. Top with chimichurri and hemp seeds.

8. Feel free to change up the vegetables. You can also top with fresh avocado.

Protein: turkey, broccoli
Fiber: all the vegetables
Healthy fat: oils

Fun Fact

Studies show parsley and cilantro *can help remove heavy metals from the body.*

Notes

Hearty Salads

1. Thai Chicken Chopped Salad

2. Taco Salad

3. Shrimp & Greens Salad

4. Pickled Veggies Salad
   w/Teriyaki Salmon

5. Gorgeous Greens & Quinoa Salad
   w/Toasted Pine Nut Dressing

Thai Chicken Chopped Salad

Servings: 4
Time: 20 minutes

Dressing

- 2 Tbsp lime juice
- 1 tsp ginger, grated
- 1 tsp red pepper flakes
- 2 Tbsp coconut sugar
- 1 tsp garlic powder
- 2 Tbsp sesame oil
- 2 Tbsp extra-virgin olive oil
- 1 Tbsp rice vinegar

The Veggies

- 2 cups green cabbage, shredded
- 2 cups Brussels sprouts, shredded
- 1 red bell pepper, diced
- 2 stalks green onions, diced
- ¼ cup basil leaves (can also use cilantro)
- 1 cup cherry tomatoes, sliced in half

Salad Toppings

- 2 cooked chicken breasts, shredded or chopped
- 1 cup cashews (roasted/salted)
- Edamame peas (out of the pod)

How it's made

1. In a measuring cup or small bowl, make the dressing by whisking together the dressing ingredients. Add sea salt and pepper if needed. Set aside.

2. In a large bowl, add all the veggies and toss. Add the dressing and toss. Put into individual serving bowls. Top each one with shredded chicken, edamame peas, and toasted cashews. Enjoy!

Protein: chicken, cashews, edamame peas
Fiber: cabbage, Brussels sprouts
Healthy fat: oils, cashews

Tips

Feel free to get creative with your vegetables. It's tasty with a little romaine lettuce and/or baby spinach. You can't go wrong with fiber-rich foods from the produce section.

Notes

Taco Salad

Servings: 4
Time: 20 minutes

Taco Bowls

- 4 brown rice tortillas (any gluten-free tortilla will work)
- Avocado oil spray (non-stick spray)

Turkey Meat

- 1lb extra-lean ground turkey
- 2 Tbsp taco seasoning (see my homemade recipe on page 201)
- 1 tsp sea salt and black pepper

Salad Add-ons

- 1 cup cherry tomatoes, cut in half
- ¼ cup cilantro, chopped
- 1 jalapeno, sliced (this is optional)
- 1 can black beans, rinsed & drained
- 1 cup thawed, frozen corn (can use canned, but drain it)
- 1 red bell pepper, diced
- 1 head romaine, chopped
- 1 avocado, sliced
- 1 lime, sliced
- Magic Green Sauce (see recipe on page 199)

How it's made

1. Preheat the oven to 375°F (190°C) and line a baking sheet with parchment paper.

2. You will need large ramekins for this (or a small oven-safe bowl). Spray each tortilla with avocado oil cooking spray. Turn the ramekin upside down and lay the tortilla over the ramekin and cover it with foil to "shape" the tortilla around the ramekin so it's a bowl shape.

3. Place the ramekins with the tortillas wrapped in foil onto the baking sheet and bake for 15 minutes. You want the ramekin upside down so the tortilla is on top.

4. Remove from the oven. Remove the foil from the tortillas and let them cool (they will harden as they cool).

5. Brown the ground turkey in a skillet over medium heat and cook completely. Add the homemade taco seasoning and sea salt. Give it a stir to combine it and remove it from the heat.

6. Time to assemble the taco bowls. I usually put the lettuce at the bottom of the serving bowls and then layer everything. You can also crush up tortilla chips and add them to the top. I always finish off with cilantro and a squeeze of lime juice.

Protein: turkey, black beans
Fiber: black beans, romaine lettuce
Healthy fat: oil from dressing, avocado

Tips

For this recipe, I really encourage you to make your own taco seasoning. Find my recipe on page 201. The store-bought taco seasoning is usually full of inflammatory junk (like MSG and a ton of sodium).

You will love the dressing recipe! Use it as a spread, a dip, or a dressing.

Shrimp & Greens Salad

Servings: 2
Time: 30 minutes

Shrimp Marinade

- 1lb shrimp, tails removed & deveined
- 1 Tbsp extra-virgin olive oil
- 1 cup orange juice, about 1 orange juiced
- ½ cup lime juice
- 4 cloves garlic, minced
- ½ shallot, finely chopped
- 2 Tbsp parsley, chopped
- ½ tsp sea salt
- ¼ tsp black pepper

Kale

- 1 cup kale leaves
- 1 tsp lime juice

Salad Add-ons

- 1 clementine orange, peeled & sectioned
- 2 cups baby spinach, roughly chopped
- 1 cup dried, unsweetened cranberries (or any dried fruit)
- 1 avocado, sliced
- ¼ cup slivered almonds

How it's made

1. In a medium bowl, whisk together the olive oil, orange juice, lime juice, garlic, shallots, parsley, sea salt, and black pepper. Add the shrimp, place in the fridge, and let them marinate for 10–20 minutes.

2. Grab the kale and tear the leaves off the vein. Rip them into bite-sized pieces and place them in a large bowl.

3. Add 1 tsp of lime juice to the kale. Put your hands in the bowl and massage the kale leaves. This will break down the cell walls of the kale. This step makes the nutrients from the kale more digestible and causes the kale to be milder in flavor.

4. Add the spinach and the clementine slices to the kale along with the dried cranberries and give it a good toss. Set in the fridge.

5. Place a skillet on the stove over medium heat. Once heated, add the shrimp and the marinade to the skillet. Place a lid on and cook for roughly 5 minutes or until the shrimp is cooked through. It should be a nice pink color. Turn off the heat and let the shrimp cool slightly.

6. Divide the lettuce mixture into serving bowls. Top with shrimp, avocado slices, and almond slivers. Now drizzle some of that shrimp juice over the bowls, squeeze a little more lime juice over them, and sprinkle with a little more sea salt. Enjoy!

Protein: shrimp
Fiber: spinach, kale
Healthy fat: avocado, extra-virgin olive oil, almonds

Tips

When buying dried fruit, be sure to read the ingredients. MOST of them are full of sugar.

Notes

Pickled Veggie Salad w/Teriyaki Salmon

Servings: 1
Time: 25 minutes

Pickled Veggies

- ½ cup rice vinegar
- 2 tsp coconut sugar
- ¼ tsp sea salt
- 1 zucchini
- 2 carrots, shredded
- ½ red onion, sliced

Salmon

- 5 oz salmon fillet
- 1 tsp avocado oil
- ½ tsp sea salt
- ¼ tsp black pepper

Teriyaki Sauce

- ½ cup tamari
- 3 Tbsp coconut sugar
- 1 Tbsp raw honey
- ½ tsp ground ginger

Salad Toppings

- ½ cup cashews, roasted/salted/chopped
- 2 Tbsp fresh parsley, chopped

How it's made

1. Heat the oven to 425°F (218°C) and line a baking sheet with parchment paper.

2. In a mixing bowl, add the rice vinegar, coconut sugar, and sea salt. Whisk until well blended. Set aside.

3. Lay the zucchini flat on a cutting board and use a peeler to slice the zucchini into thin strips.

4. Now add the sliced zucchini, shredded carrots, and sliced red onion to the vinegar mixture and stir to coat all the vegetables. Set aside and let them marinate (pickle) while you prepare the salmon.

5. Pat dry your salmon and rub the avocado oil, sea salt, and black pepper to coat the salmon fillets. Place them skin-side down on the baking sheet.

6. In a small measuring cup, whisk together the tamari, coconut sugar, honey, garlic, and ginger. Pour the mixture over the salmon fillets.

7. Cook the salmon for 6–7 minutes and remove it from the oven. Remove the skin from each fillet after they cool for 2 minutes.

8. Place the pickled veggies on serving plates, top with the cooked salmon, and finish them off with crushed (roasted) cashews and fresh parsley. Enjoy!

Protein: salmon, cashews
Fiber: zucchini
Healthy fat: salmon, avocado oil

Notes

Gorgeous Greens & Quinoa Salad w/Toasted Pine Nut Dressing

Servings: 4
Time: 30 minutes

Greens Mixture

- 3 cups broccoli (about 2 florets)
- 1 cup baby spinach
- ¼ cup fresh parsley
- 1 Tbsp nutritional yeast
- 1 Tbsp Italian seasoning
- ⅛ tsp chili flakes (a pinch)
- 1 tsp sea salt
- ½ tsp black pepper
- 1 tsp avocado oil
- ½ shallot, diced
- 3 garlic cloves, minced

Dressing

- 3 Tbsp unsweetened non-dairy yogurt (cashew milk yogurt is my favorite)
- 2 Tbsp lemon juice
- ¼ tsp sea salt
- ½ cup pine nuts
- ¼ cup extra-virgin olive oil

Salad Add-ons

- 2 carrots, shredded
- 1 Tbsp lemon juice
- ½ cup dried unsweetened cranberries (or any dried fruit)
- 2 cups quinoa, cooked

How it's made

1. In a large (dry) skillet on low heat, toast the pine nuts for 3–4 minutes. Remove the pan from the heat. Take them out of the pan and set aside. You want them to just start turning a light brown. They burn fast, so watch closely. Take three-quarters of the pine nuts and chop them very finely. I like to use a coffee grinder or a mini chopper. Save one-quarter of the pine nuts for the salad topper.

2. In a food processor or blender, add the broccoli florets, spinach, parsley, nutritional yeast, Italian seasoning, chili flakes, sea salt, and black pepper. Roughly chop it all (pulsing is best).

3. In the same pan you used for the pine nuts, heat some avocado oil on low heat. Add the diced shallot and cook until translucent and fragrant. Add the minced garlic and heat for 30 seconds.

4. Add the chopped vegetable mixture to the pan and stir. Cover and cook on low for 10 minutes or until the veggies cook down and are soft.

5. While the vegetables are cooking, make your dressing. In a bowl, whisk together the yogurt, half the lemon juice, the chopped pine nuts, and a pinch of sea salt. Now slowly whisk in the olive oil, whisking continuously so the oil blends with the mixture. Set aside.

6. Add the shredded carrots and remaining lemon juice to the vegetable mixture and cook for another 2 minutes. Remove from the heat and add the dried fruit and cooked quinoa. Give it all a good stir.

7. Serve with a dollop of the dressing and top with remaining pine nuts and parsley.

Protein: quinoa, pine nuts, yogurt, broccoli, nutritional yeast
Fiber: broccoli, baby spinach
Healthy fat: oils, pine nuts

Tips

For added protein you can top the salad with a piece of baked salmon or chicken breast

To speed up cooking time, make your quinoa at the beginning of the week during your meal prepping. I usually make 1-2 cups a week. It's better left over anyway!

Fun Fact

Quinoa *is a complete protein, just like any animal protein.*

Notes

Let's Talk About Oils!

I talk about oils a lot... but I don't think I can ever talk about them enough. If you think about it, oils are in almost everything we eat. We cook with them, make dressings with them, bake with them, and they are in ninety percent of the processed foods we buy today, from crackers to salad dressings and nut butters to canned nuts. From frozen dinners to cookies. Let's face it, we consume a lot of oil.

There are oils that are really nutritious, though. They provide healthy fats for our body and can be very anti-inflammatory. On the contrary, there are also refined oils, which aren't good for us at all and are super inflammatory.

I believe when we know better, we do better so let me break it down for you. That way, you're able to make healthier choices the next time you go grocery shopping.

What are refined oils?

Refined oils are usually chemically extracted from a plant or seed. They use a harsh chemical to get the oil out of the plant. Then it goes through a nine-step process to become oil on the grocery store shelf. Three of these steps involve bleaching and deodorizing. Now, I'm no rocket scientist, but the words "bleaching" and "deodorizing" are not ones I want to describe the food I put into my body. Refined oils are basically filled with chemicals, put into a clear/plastic bottle, have eternal shelf lives, and are VERY inflammatory.

The scary part is most of the processed foods today are made with these refined oils. Here are the big ones, the ones you will see the most, and the ones you really need to watch out for:

- Canola oil
- Palm oil
- Sunflower oil
- Vegetable oil

There are more, but these are the most common ones found in processed foods like nut butters, sauces, crackers, and more.

Enough of the bad news. Let's talk about the good guys!

Three favorite oils to use in my kitchen are:

- Coconut oil
- Avocado oil
- Extra-virgin olive oil

They are all easy to find, anti-inflammatory, and contain good, quality healthy fats.

Oils are sensitive!

Oils are light AND heat sensitive, so it matters when and how you use the different oils in your recipes. Oils have what they call a "smoke point." That smoke point is a measuring system for how much heat an oil can withstand before it starts to break down.

Extra-virgin olive oil (EVOO) does NOT like a lot of heat, so it isn't ideal to use over the stove when cooking food. I save this oil for dressings, marinades, sauces, and drizzling (YUMMO).

Avocado oil LOVES heat. That is why I use it in all my sauté dishes. It is also mild in flavor so you can bake with it too.

Coconut oil likes heat. This is my go-to for baking and desserts. I also throw a scoop of coconut oil into my smoothies for added healthy fat.

Here's your takeaways

Choose your oils depending on how much heat the recipe calls for.

Buy oils in dark glass containers because they don't like a lot of light.

Read your processed food labels (the ingredient list) to start recognizing those pesky refined oils. Keep in mind, refined oils are very affordable which makes packaging the food cheaper. There are great brands out there that use good oils. You just have to seek them out.

Soups

1. Instant Pot Leek & Potato Soup w/Kale
2. Broccoli Cheesy Potato Soup
3. Chicken Tortilla Soup
4. White Chicken Chili
5. Turkey Cabbage Soup

Instant Pot Leek & Potato Soup w/Kale

Servings: 4
Time: 1 hour

- 1 cup cashews
- 1½ cups hot water
- 4 cups vegetable broth
- 2 leeks (white parts only) finely chopped
- 2 stalks celery, diced
- 1 cup green cabbage (chopped)
- 4 garlic cloves, minced
- 1 tsp dried oregano
- ¼ tsp dried thyme
- 1 tsp sea salt
- 2 yellow potatoes, diced medium-sized
- 2 cups kale leaves, stems removed, chopped
- 2 Tbsp lemon juice
- 2 Tbsp fresh dill, chopped (optional)

How it's made

1. Place your cashews in very hot water and let them soak for at least 20 minutes. Prepare all your vegetables while they soak.

2. Turn your pressure cooker to sauté mode and add half a cup of vegetable broth. Add the leeks, celery, and cabbage, and cook for 4–5 minutes until softened. Add the garlic, oregano, thyme, and sea salt and stir to combine, cooking for 1 minute more.

3. Turn off the sauté mode and add the potatoes along with the remaining vegetable broth. Stir to combine. Put the lid on and set it to "sealing," then press manual/pressure cooker and cook for 10 minutes on high pressure. Once finished cooking, turn off and do a quick release.

4. Remove about three-quarters of the soup and place in a blender along with the soaked cashews. Carefully blend to purée until smooth. Pour this back into the pressure cooker. Add the kale leaves and lemon juice and stir. Place the lid on the instant pot to allow the soup to heat through and let the kale wilt a little. Divide into bowls, garnish with dill if using, and enjoy!

Protein: cashews
Fiber: kale, celery, leeks
Healthy fat: cashews

Notes

Cheesy Broccoli Potato Soup

Servings: 4
Time: 40 minutes

- 1 cup cashews
- 2 cups hot water
- 1 Tbsp avocado oil
- 1 tsp turmeric
- ½ tsp paprika
- ½ tsp onion powder
- 3 carrots, diced
- 1 yellow onion, diced small
- 2 russet potatoes, peeled/diced
- 3 garlic cloves, minced
- 6 cups vegetable broth (divided)
- 1 tsp sea salt
- ½ tsp black pepper
- 2 Tbsp nutritional yeast
- 1 Tbsp lemon juice
- 3 cups broccoli, finely chopped
- 2 stalks green onions, diced

How it's made

1. In a small bowl, soak your cashews in hot water and set aside. Let them soak for at least 30 minutes to soften. I usually cover mine to help the steam stay trapped.

2. In a soup pot over low heat, add the avocado oil. Once it's hot, add the turmeric, paprika, and onion powder. Just mix them in the oil and let them cook for about 30 seconds. This activates their flavors.

3. Add the diced onion and carrots. Cook until onions are translucent. Add the minced garlic and cook for 1 more minute.

4. Add the diced potatoes, 5 cups of the broth, sea salt, and black pepper. Turn up the heat and bring to a boil. Stir really well and place a lid on the pot. Lower heat and slow simmer the soup until the potatoes are cooked. If they are small chunks, it should only take about 15 minutes.

5. Drain and rinse the cashews and place them in a high-speed blender. Add the remaining vegetable broth and give them a blend until super smooth. It usually takes about 2 minutes. This is going to make your soup creamy without using dairy.

6. Once your potatoes are cooked, turn off the heat to the soup. Let it cool for a few minutes. With a slotted spoon, remove half of the vegetables from the soup pot and place them in the blender along with your blended cashews. Add the nutritional yeast, lemon juice, and more sea salt and black pepper if needed. Blend until creamy. If it's too thick, add more broth.

7. While that blends, add the finely chopped broccoli florets to the soup pot and stir. Turn the heat back on super low. We don't need to cook anything. We are just keeping everything warm. Now add the blender mixture to your soup pot. Give it all a good stir and heat the soup until everything is warm and well blended.

8. Place into serving bowls, top with green onions, and enjoy!

Protein: cashews, broccoli, nutritional yeast
Fiber: carrots, broccoli
Healthy fat: avocado oil, cashews

Tips

If you want the soup to be really creamy, simply place all the soup mixture in the blender (in batches) and add the broccoli once you put the mixture back in the soup pot.

Be sure to crack the lid on your blender. The steam needs to escape.

Fun Fact

Turmeric is very anti-inflammatory. *It's mild in flavor and it's bright yellow in color so I add it to any "yellow" dish like squash, salmon, etc.*

Notes

Chicken Tortilla Soup

Servings: 4
Time: 5 hours

For the Soup

- 1lb chicken thighs
- Taco seasoning (see my homemade recipe on page 201)
- 1 bay leaf
- 1 yellow onion, diced
- 1 red bell pepper, diced
- 1 can fire-roasted diced tomatoes (undrained)
- 1 can Rotel (undrained)
- 1 x 4 oz can green chilies
- 1 can black beans, drained/rinsed
- 2 cups frozen corn
- 4 cups chicken broth
- 1 tsp sea salt
- 1 cup kale leaves, stems removed/chopped
- ½ cup cilantro, chopped
- ¼ cup lime juice (juice of 2 limes)

For the Tortilla Strips

- 6 corn tortillas
- 1 tsp avocado oil cooking spray
- ½ tsp sea salt

Soup Add-ons

- Avocado, sliced
- 1 bunch of cilantro, chopped

How it's made

1. Place your chicken thighs in the crockpot and rub them with the taco seasoning, coating them really well.

2. In the crockpot add the bay leaf, onions, bell peppers, tomatoes, green chilies, black beans, corn, and sea salt. Mix it all around and pour the chicken broth over it.

3. Cover and cook on low for 5 hours. Stir every couple of hours.

4. While the soup cooks, let's make the tortilla strips. Heat your oven to 375°F (190°C) and line a baking sheet with parchment paper.

5. Stack your corn tortillas and cut vertical lines through the strips and then cut those strips in half. Spread them on a baking sheet and give them a light spray of non-stick cooking spray. I use avocado oil cooking spray. Sprinkle them with salt and cook for 7–9 minutes (or until they start turning brown). Set them aside.

6. During the last hour of cooking your soup, take out the chicken thighs, shred them, and put them back into the crockpot. Add the chopped kale and cilantro. Cover and let the soup continue cooking.

7. Serve with lime juice and top with avocado chunks, more cilantro, and tortilla strips. Enjoy!

Protein: chicken, black beans
Fiber: kale
Healthy fat: avocado

Notes

White Chicken Chili

Servings: 8
Time: 30 minutes

- 1½ lbs chicken thighs
- 1 yellow onion, diced
- 1 can green chilies
- 1 tsp cumin
- ½ tsp coriander
- ¼ tsp oregano
- 2 cans chickpeas, rinsed/drained
- 4 cups chicken broth
- 3 Tbsp lime juice (juice of half a lime)
- 1 Tbsp avocado oil
- 1 cup frozen corn
- 1 avocado (sliced, optional)
- ⅓ cup cilantro (chopped)
- Sea salt & black pepper (to taste)
- ½ cup water

How it's made

1. Place the avocado oil in a Dutch oven or soup pot and turn heat to medium low. Add the diced onion and cook until translucent.

2. Add the green chilies and stir to combine. Add in 1 can of drained/rinsed chickpeas. Add in the cumin, coriander, and oregano. Place your chicken thighs on top (be sure to rinse and pat the chicken dry). Cook on medium-low until chicken is no longer pink on the outside. Add more oil if the chicken begins to stick.

3. Add the chicken broth. Place the lid on the pot and simmer for 15–20 minutes (the chicken needs to be cooked through).

4. While it cooks, add the other can of chickpeas (rinsed and drained) to a blender with water to make a creamy paste. Set aside.

5. Take the cooked chicken thighs out and shred the chicken. Place it back in the pot along with the creamy chickpea mixture.

6. Add the cilantro and corn. Let the soup simmer on low for 5–10 minutes. Add sea salt and black pepper to taste. Place in individual bowls and top with fresh avocado, more lime juice, and extra cilantro if desired. Enjoy!

Protein: chicken, chickpeas, chicken broth
Healthy fat: avocados, avocado oil

Tip

To add a kick, feel free to add fresh jalapeno slices.

Notes

_____

_____

_____

_____

_____

_____

_____

_____

_____

Turkey Cabbage Soup

Servings: 4
Time: 30 minutes

- 1lb extra-lean ground turkey
- 1 yellow onion, chopped
- 3 garlic cloves, minced
- ½ tsp dried thyme
- 2 Tbsp tomato paste
- 8 cups chicken broth
- 2 cups diced tomatoes, undrained
- 3 cups green cabbage, chopped
- 3 medium carrots, diced
- 2 cups kale leaves, chopped
- 2 Tbsp lime juice
- 1 red bell pepper, diced
- ½ tsp sea salt
- ¼ tsp black pepper
- 2 Tbsp fresh parsley (for garnish)

How it's made

1. In a soup pot, heat the avocado oil on medium-low heat and add the diced onions. Cook until translucent.

2. Add the ground turkey and cook until no longer pink. Stir in the garlic, thyme, and tomato paste and cook for another minute.

3. Add the broth and diced tomatoes and stir to combine. Now add the cabbage and carrots. Bring the soup to a gentle boil then reduce heat to a low simmer for 10 minutes.

4. Now add in the kale, bell pepper, and season with sea salt and black pepper. Cook for an additional 10 minutes. Squeeze in the lime and put into serving bowls. Top with fresh parsley and enjoy!

Protein: turkey, chicken broth
Fiber: cabbage, kale
Vitamin C: bell pepper, carrot

Tip

Other great vegetable options include zucchini (add them at the end because they cook fast), mushrooms, bok choy, and leeks.

Notes

Vegetarian Dishes

1. Chipotle Lime Cauliflower Lettuce Wraps
2. You Name it! Green & Protein Chop
3. Crispy Baked Sesame Tofu
4. Spiced Cauliflower Quinoa Bowl
5. Gluten-Free Lo Mein

Chipotle Lime Cauliflower Lettuce Wraps

Servings: 4
Time: 30 minutes

For the Cauliflower

- 1 head cauliflower (broken into florets)
- 1 x 7 oz can chipotle in adobo
- ¼ cup raw honey

For the Dressing

- 3 Tbsp raw honey
- 3 Tbsp lime juice
- 3 Tbsp extra-virgin olive oil
- 1 tsp cilantro, chopped

Wrap Add-ons

- 1 head Boston lettuce (can also use romaine)
- 1 cup cooked quinoa
- 1 avocado, diced
- 1 carrot, shredded
- 1 Tbsp cilantro, chopped

How it's made

1. Preheat the oven to 375°F (190°C) and line a baking sheet with parchment paper.

2. Open the can of chipotles and place them in a bowl with the sauce from the can. Remove the peppers and chop them. Place them back with the sauce from the can and add 1 Tbsp of honey. Give it all a good mix and set it side.

3. Roll the cauliflower florets in the chipotle mixture and place them on the baking sheet. Cook for 25 minutes or until the cauliflower is cooked through.

4. Boston lettuce, also called butter lettuce, is super delicate and creamy. If you aren't using it, you can use romaine leaves. Remove the leaves from the head of lettuce. Set aside.

5. Make your dressing by adding the remaining honey, extra-virgin olive oil, a pinch of the chopped cilantro, and lime juice to a bowl and whisk until well combined.

6. To assemble the lettuce wraps, place your lettuce leaves on a plate. Add the cooked cauliflower, cooked quinoa, diced avocado, cilantro, green onions, and top with the dressing. Squeeze some additional lime and enjoy!

Healthy fat: extra-virgin olive oil, avocado
Fiber: lettuce, cauliflower
Protein: quinoa

Notes

You Name it! Green & Protein Chop

Servings: 4
Time: 15 minutes

For the Salad

- ½ cup quinoa
- 1 cup vegetable broth
- 2 cups baby spinach
- 1 cup romaine
- ½ cup green cabbage
- ¼ cup cilantro
- 1 cup broccoli

For the Dressing

- ¼ cup extra-virgin olive oil
- 2 Tbsp lemon juice
- 2 Tbsp red wine vinegar
- ½ tsp garlic powder
- ½ tsp sea salt
- ¼ tsp black pepper
- 2 Tbsp raw honey

Salad Add-ons

- 1 can chickpeas, rinsed/drained
- 1 stalk green onion, diced by hand
- ¼ cup pumpkin seeds, toasted/salted

How it's made

1. To cook the quinoa, heat a small saucepan on medium and add the vegetable broth and quinoa. When it begins to boil, turn the heat to low, put on a lid, and cook for 6-7 minutes or until the liquid has evaporated. In a pinch, you can use water instead of vegetable broth. Remove from the heat and let it cool completely.

2. Take all the leafy greens, cilantro, and broccoli and add them to a food processor. This makes for fast chopping. You can hand chop if you don't have a food processor. You will want to dice the green onion by hand.

3. To make the dressing, mix together the olive oil, lemon juice, vinegar, garlic powder, sea salt, pepper, and honey. Use a whisk to get it all well combined.

4. In a large bowl add in the chopped vegetables, green onion, chickpeas, quinoa, and pumpkin seeds. Toss.

Protein: quinoa, chickpeas
Fiber: all the greens
Healthy fat: extra-virgin olive oil

Tips

Feel free to create your own version of this. Here are some additional ideas: kale, cucumber, parsley, cashews, almonds, and dried fruit. The goal is to keep it as green as possible. Don't substitute the chickpeas or the quinoa. They are your protein source.

Unless you are eating all the salad in one meal, do not put the dressing in the big bowl. Place the salad into individual serving bowls and add the dressing to those. You can then save the leftover dry salad for another meal. Enjoy!

Notes

Crispy Baked Sesame Tofu

Servings: 3
Time: 30 minutes

For the Tofu

- 1lb tofu (extra firm)
- 1 Tbsp tamari
- 1 Tbsp arrowroot powder (or tapioca flour)
- ½ cup cashews
- 1 tsp sea salt
- ¼ tsp garlic powder
- ½ tsp sesame oil
- 1 Tbsp sesame seeds

For the Sauce

- ½ cup tamari
- ⅓ cup coconut sugar
- 2 Tbsp Mirin (or rice vinegar)
- ¼ cup white cooking wine
- 2 tsp arrowroot powder (or tapioca starch)
- 1 Tbsp water

Tofu Add-ons

- 2 stalks green onions, diced
- 1 Tbsp sesame seeds

How it's made

1. Preheat the oven to 425°F (218°C). In a food processor, mini chopper, or coffee grinder, chop your cashews very fine and set them aside.

2. It's important to get all the moisture out of the tofu. Place the block between paper towels and press. Keep repeating this until all the water is out of the tofu. Cut into cubes.

3. In a small bowl, combine arrowroot powder, tamari, and crushed cashews (or your nuts of choice). Add the cubed tofu and toss to coat. Add the sesame seeds and toss them again.

4. Place the tofu on a parchment-lined baking sheet. Spread them apart so they aren't touching. This will help them stay crispy. Bake for 20 minutes.

5. While the tofu is baking, heat a small saucepan and add the tamari, coconut sugar, and mirin (or rice wine vinegar). Whisking often. Bring to a gentle boil, lower heat and keep whisking so the sugar dissolves and to ensure the sauce doesn't stick. Continue to cook and whisk until the sauce is reduced and coats a spoon. Remove from heat and let cool for 2–3 minutes.

6. Remove the tofu from the oven and place it in a bowl. In a small dish combine the arrowroot powder and water and whisk until dissolved. Add this slurry to the sauce and stir. Pour the sauce over the tofu and stir to coat. Top them with green onions and sesame seeds. Serve with brown rice or quinoa.

Protein: tofu, cashews, sesame seeds
Healthy fat: sesame oil

Tip

You don't need to be vegetarian or vegan to enjoy tofu. It's a good source of protein. We should all give our bodies a break from animal protein every so often.

Notes

Spiced Cauliflower Quinoa Bowl

Servings: 2
Time: 40 minutes

For the Quinoa

- ⅔ cup quinoa (uncooked)
- ¼ tsp sea salt
- ¼ tsp black pepper

For the Cauliflower

- ½ head cauliflower, cut into florets
- ¼ tsp turmeric
- ½ tsp paprika
- ½ tsp dried thyme

For the Sauce

- 2 Tbsp tahini
- 1 garlic clove, minced
- 1 Tbsp lemon juice
- ½ tsp tamari
- 1 Tbsp water

Bowl Add-ons

- 1 avocado, sliced
- ¼ cup cilantro, chopped
- 1 tsp sesame seeds

How it's made

1. Preheat the oven to 400°F (204°C) and line a baking sheet with parchment paper.

2. Cook the quinoa according to the directions on the package. Once cooked, fluff with a fork and season with sea salt and black pepper. Set it aside.

3. While the quinoa cooks, add the cauliflower to a medium-sized bowl and toss with the turmeric, paprika, and thyme. I usually mix up the spices first in the bowl and then toss the florets around in the mixed spices. Place them on the baking sheet and bake for 30 to 35 minutes or until fork tender

4. In a small bowl whisk together the tahini, garlic, lemon juice, tamari, and water. Set aside.

5. Divide the quinoa between serving bowls and top with cauliflower, avocado, cilantro, and sesame seeds. Drizzle the tahini dressing over top. Enjoy!

Protein: tahini, sesame seeds
Fiber: cauliflower
Healthy fat: avocado

Fun Fact

Tahini is made from sesame seeds *like peanut butter is made from peanuts. Tahini is a great alternative for those with nut allergies.*

Notes

Gluten-free Lo Mein

Servings: 2
Time: 20 minutes

For the Lo Mein

- 8 oz gluten-free ramen (or any gluten-free noodle)
- 1 piece kombu (optional but oh-so-good for you)
- 2 Tbsp sesame oil (divided)
- 1 Tbsp avocado oil
- 3 stalks green onions, chopped
- 4 carrots, diced
- 1½ cups green cabbage, chopped
- 1 head broccoli (cut into florets)
- 1 cup mushrooms, stems removed/diced
- 2 Tbsp Mirin (or rice vinegar)

For the Miso Slurry

- 1 Tbsp miso paste
- 1 Tbsp water

For the Sauce

- 2 Tbsp lime juice
- ½ tsp sea salt
- ¼ tsp black pepper
- 2 garlic cloves, minced
- 1 Tbsp raw honey
- 2 Tbsp tamari

Bowl Add-ons

- 1 Tbsp sesame seeds

How it's made

1. Cook noodles according to package directions and add a piece of Kombu to the water. Once noodles are cooked, discard the kombu and throw it away. Be sure to rinse your pasta. Gluten-free pasta needs to be rinsed or it will be very sticky.

2. In a large sauté pan, heat half the sesame oil and the avocado oil on medium-low heat. Add the onion and sauté for 2 minutes. Now add the remaining vegetables and toss. Cook for about 5 minutes or until they soften but still have some firmness.

3. While the vegetables are cooking, add the miso and water to a small bowl and smash/whisk until a paste forms.

4. In a measuring cup or small bowl, mix the miso slurry along with the other half of the sesame oil, garlic, honey, tamari, sea salt, and black pepper. Whisk well and set aside.

5. To the vegetable mixture, add the Mirin and give it all a good stir (you can also use rice vinegar if you don't have Mirin, but it may need a little more honey as Mirin is a little sweet).

6. Add in the cooked noodles and half the sauce and stir well. Add in the rest of the sauce and sauté on low for 1–2 minutes. Turn the heat off and add in the lime juice and top with sesame seeds.

Protein: chickpea pasta, broccoli, miso paste, sesame seeds
Fiber: cabbage, broccoli
Healthy fat: sesame oil, avocado oil

Tip

If you want to add animal protein, I would suggest chicken thighs (cut into cubes). Toss them in a little bit of oil and sea salt. You will cook them first and remove them from the pan. Then follow the steps and add the chicken back in with the pasta.

Fun Fact

Kombu is a form of seaweed. *Seaweed is a superfood. By adding it to your pasta water, you are allowing that pasta to soak in all those minerals from the sea. It's virtually tasteless. I recommend adding it to any soup you make. Just discard it before serving (like you do with bay leaves).*

Notes

What Brought Me Here

I t was fall of 2013. I had been married for about six months, I was working full-time at Capital One Bank, and my new husband and I had also opened up two retail locations that our son ran but we still owned, which involved payroll, marketing, accounting, product ordering, customer service, online sales, and so on.

Capital One did a massive layoff, and I was one of the victims. It was a blessing in disguise because I was burning the candle at both ends and Neil's candles were up in flames as he juggled a full-time construction company AND the retail stores.

Fast forward to February 2014. Neil had a heart attack on Super Bowl Sunday. He survived and when we got a second shot at life together, we re-evaluated our lives and decided to make massive change. We sold our retail businesses, sold our home, sold most of our belongings, bought an RV and planned a one-way trip to Florida.

We took off in August of 2015 and had a three-month RV trip planned along the entire coast of Florida. I'm talking Destin down to Naples, across Florida, down to the Keys, and back up the east coast. We landed in Juno Beach, Florida, and fell in love so we stayed there for the next six or seven months.

That is when I really began to sit still and listen. I listened to myself think for the first time in my entire life. I slowed down enough to really put my life into perspective. I didn't know it at the time, but having these months in Florida, surrounded by strangers and the beautiful ocean, allowed me the space to just be. Be with my body. Be with my thoughts. Relax. Sleep as much as I wanted. Exercise every day...OUTSIDE. My biggest daily decision consisted of "Will I walk with the dogs or ride my bike today?" It was magical.

When we decided to move back to Texas, I really had a hard time adjusting. I was jobless but also right back in the place I had lived my entire life. BORING. Looking back, I would definitely say depression started kicking in. I yearned for purpose. I wanted so badly to start something new, and I knew I wanted to help people. I wanted to serve.

I did some volunteering at a food bank, and I also got a part-time job at a flower shop. Creating beautiful flower arrangements really put a smile on my face. That was until I had to deal with retail life and the drama that was conducted with the employees. I don't do drama, so I left after about six months. To this day, I still enjoy a beautifully crafted flower arrangement. That work isn't easy.

During the first few months of moving back to Texas, I stumbled upon The Institute for Integrative Nutrition and I was immediately drawn in. I wanted to learn how we could live a more holistic lifestyle so that Neil could get off the medication he was taking. This is where my life changed. This is the moment I really started finding my purpose in life.

I had such a passion for knowledge. I found something I really loved, getting healthy in the most natural way. I used food. I learned how to treat food and how well it could treat me if I made some small changes. I gained clarity on my path and my purpose one lesson at a time.

Six years and three schools later, the rest is history. I now teach others how to create a healthier lifestyle through food. Food is everything and if more people can just learn how food directly affects their health, this world would be in a much better state, mentally and physically.

It doesn't require massive change or an overhaul of your refrigerator. It just takes small steps that create habits. Those habits begin to shift your health in a positive direction. Knowing what you are eating is the biggest step. I teach people how to pull the curtain back on their food products and see what is really in them. Crafting a healthy recipe that is also delicious is so fun for me, which is why this cookbook exists today.

It all started with a heart attack and a very low point in my life. 2014 was a rough year with many deaths, family tragedies, and life-threatening health scares. But I chose to turn it into something beautiful. And now I am helping others turn their lives into something beautiful by being healthier and that makes me smile.

Yard Bird
(aka Poultry)

1. Pesto Chicken Stuffed Peppers
2. Chicken & Broccoli Casserole
3. Greek Chicken Sliders w/Tzatziki Tapenade
4. Turkey Meatballs w/Coconut Curry Rice

Pesto Chicken Stuffed Peppers

Servings: 6
Time: 30 minutes

- 3 red bell peppers (cut in half lengthwise, seeds removed)
- 2 Tbsp water
- 2 large chicken breasts
- ½ cup quinoa, cooked
- 1 cup Dairy-free Pesto (see my recipe on page 197)
- 1 broccoli head, finely chopped
- 2 stalks green onions, diced
- 3 garlic cloves, minced
- 2 Tbsp nutritional yeast
- 2 Tbsp lemon juice
- ½ tsp sea salt
- ¼ tsp black pepper
- 2 Tbsp vegan Parmesan (optional)

How it's made

1. Cook the chicken breast to your liking. Here is how I do it. Place the breasts in the instant pot with 1 cup of chicken broth. Salt and pepper the breasts. Close the lid and pressure cook them on high for 15 minutes. Remove them and shred the chicken.

2. Preheat the oven to 375°F (190°C). In a baking dish, add the water and place the bell pepper halves (cut side down) in the dish. Cover with foil and bake for 8–10 minutes. This will soften the peppers slightly.

3. While the peppers are cooking, add the cooked/shredded chicken to a large bowl, quinoa, pesto, broccoli, green onions, garlic, nutritional yeast, lemon juice, sea salt, and black pepper. Give it all a good mix.

4. Once you take the peppers out of the oven, discard the water, and place the peppers cut side up so you can stuff them. Place the mixture evenly in the pepper holes. Top with vegan Parmesan cheese if you are using it, place them in the oven and bake for 15–20 minutes. Enjoy!

Protein: chicken, nutritional yeast, quinoa, broccoli
Fiber: broccoli, greens in pesto sauce
Healthy fat: oils in pesto

Tips

We use the chicken mixture in this recipe for other recipes. Double it and you can eat it throughout the week.

Any color bell peppers will work.

Notes

Chicken & Broccoli Casserole

Servings: 4
Time: 45 minutes

For the Chicken

- Gluten-free spaghetti
- 1lb chicken thighs (boneless, skinless, cut into small pieces)
- 1 tsp sea salt (divided)
- 2 tsp avocado oil
- 5 cups broccoli (cut into florets)
- 3 carrots, diced
- ½ yellow onion, thinly sliced

For the Sauce

- 1¼ cups organic coconut milk (full fat, from the can)
- 2 Tbsp nutritional yeast
- ½ tsp garlic powder
- 1 Tbsp lemon juice
- 1 tsp sea salt
- 1 Tbsp tapioca flour (replaces cornstarch)
- 1 Tbsp water

How it's made

1. Preheat the oven to 375°F (190°C).

2. Cook your pasta according to package directions. Drain it, rinse it, and set aside.

3. Season the chicken thigh pieces with half of the sea salt. Heat a skillet over medium heat and add the avocado oil. Working in batches, add the chicken and cook for 6-7 minutes per side or until cooked through. Remove the chicken and set aside to cool. Once cool, shred the chicken with two forks.

4. In the same skillet, using the fat from the chicken, add broccoli, carrot, yellow onion, and sea salt. Cook for 3-4 minutes until the broccoli is bright green & carrots begin to soften. Remove from the pan.

5. Meanwhile, in a saucepan over medium-low heat, add the coconut milk, nutritional yeast, garlic powder, lemon juice and remaining sea salt. Whisk to combine.

6. While the sauce is heating, in a small bowl combine the tapioca flour (or arrowroot powder) with the water and whisk to dissolve. This is called a slurry.

7. Once the sauce begins to boil, turn off the heat and add in the slurry and whisk to combine. It will slowly thicken.

8. Add the chicken thighs to an oven-safe dish and top with the broccoli mixture, and cooked pasta. Add the sauce on top and give it a stir. Place it in the oven and bake for 20 minutes. Remove, let it cool slightly, and then serve. Enjoy!

Protein: chicken, broccoli, nutritional yeast
Fiber: broccoli
Healthy fat: avocado oil, coconut milk

Tip

Be sure to buy full-fat coconut milk. Our bodies need good/healthy fat. To make "low-fat" coconut milk, they remove the good fat and put cornstarch back in the can to thicken it back up.

Notes

Greek Chicken Sliders w/Tzatziki Tapenade

Servings: 8
Time: 45 minutes

- 1½ tsp extra-virgin olive oil
- 1 red bell pepper, diced and divided
- ½ cup red onion, diced and divided
- 1lb extra-lean ground chicken
- ½ cup black olives, chopped and divided
- ½ cup pitted Kalamata olives, chopped and divided
- 4 cups baby spinach
- 1 cup almond flour
- ¼ tsp onion powder
- ½ tsp oregano
- ¼ tsp garlic powder
- 2 Tbsp lemon juice, divided
- ½ tsp fresh dill, chopped & divided
- ½ tsp sea salt
- ¼ tsp black pepper
- ½ cup unsweetened coconut yogurt (or any non-dairy unsweetened yogurt)
- ½ cucumber, diced
- 1 tomato, diced
- 2 cloves garlic, minced
- 4 cups mixed greens (or baby spinach)

How it's made

1. Preheat the oven to 400°F (204°C). Skip this step if you are grilling the sliders. Heat olive oil in a large skillet over medium heat.

2. Add half of the red pepper and half of the red onion to the skillet. Sauté for about 5 minutes or until the onion is translucent. Add baby spinach and stir until just barely wilted. Remove from heat and set aside to cool.

3. Add almond flour, ground chicken, half of the black olives, and half of the kalamata olives to the mixing bowl. Add in the garlic powder, onion powder, lemon juice, oregano, and half the dill. Now add in your sauteed vegetables. Mix well. Form the mixture into even patties and place them on a parchment-lined baking sheet. Transfer to the fridge until ready to bake or grill.

4. Meanwhile, create your tzatziki tapenade in a bowl by combining the remaining red pepper, red onion, black olives, kalamata olives, dill, yogurt, lemon juice, garlic, and cucumber. Drizzle with a splash of extra-virgin olive oil and season with sea salt and pepper to taste. Set aside.

5. If you are baking them, place them in a preheated oven for 12–15 minutes or until the internal temp is 165 F or preheat the grill over medium heat. Transfer burgers onto the grill and cook for about 7–8 minutes per side or until the burger is cooked through. Remove from the grill or oven.

6. Plate burger (or burgers) over a bed of greens (or spinach) and top with your tzatziki tapenade. Enjoy!

Protein: chicken, almond flour
Fiber: greens, bell pepper
Healthy fat: oil

Notes

Turkey Meatballs with Coconut Curry Rice

Servings: 4
Time: 25 minutes

For the Meatballs

- 1 egg
- 1 Tbsp tamari
- 1 tsp sesame oil
- 2 garlic cloves, minced
- 3 Tbsp cilantro, chopped
- 2 tsp sea salt
- 1 Tbsp sesame seeds (black or white)
- 1 tsp paprika
- ½ tsp curry powder
- 1lb extra-lean ground turkey (can use chicken)
- 1 cup ground almonds (or any nut)

For the Sauce

- 1 tsp sesame oil
- 2 cloves garlic, minced
- 3 Tbsp cilantro, chopped
- 1 tsp sea salt
- 1 cup canned coconut milk (full fat)
- 2 Tbsp Thai red curry paste
- ½ tsp fresh ginger, grated
- ½ tsp red pepper flakes
- 2 stalks green onions (diced)

For the Rice

- 2 cups jasmine rice (uncooked)
- 1 can coconut milk
- 1½ cups water
- 1 tsp sea salt
- 1 tsp fresh ginger, grated

How it's made

1. Heat the oven to 400°F and line a baking sheet with parchment paper or a silicone mat.

2. In a bowl, whisk your egg. Now add the tamari, half the cilantro, half the sesame oil, half the sea salt, half the minced garlic, sesame seeds, paprika, and curry. Once that is mixed, add the ground turkey and crushed nuts. Give it a good mix. I like to put on rubber gloves and use my hands to get this mixture well combined. You can also use a large spoon. If the mixture isn't dry enough, add more crushed nuts. If the mixture is too dry, add a little more tamari or sesame oil.

3. Take a melon baller (or you can use your hands and eye it) and make even-sized meatballs. Set aside.

4. In a crockpot, add in the remaining sesame oil, garlic, ginger, coconut milk, red curry paste, red pepper flakes, and the remaining chopped cilantro, minced garlic, and sea salt. Use a whisk to combine everything. Now place your meatballs in the sauce, turn the crockpot on low and cook for 4–5 hours.

5. While your meatballs are cooking, prepare the rice by rinsing it thoroughly using a sieve and drain.

6. Open the can of coconut milk and stir it. The cream has probably separated from the water so give it a good mix. In a medium saucepan, bring the coconut milk, water, salt, and ground ginger to a gentle boil. Add the rice and lower to a simmer.

7. Cover with a lid and simmer for 15–20 minutes, or until the liquid has evaporated. Try not to lift the lid. Remove from the heat and let it sit for 10 minutes.

Protein: turkey, crushed almonds
Healthy fat: coconut milk, almonds

Notes

From The Sea
(aka Seafood Dishes)

1. Cilantro Lime Shrimp Skillet

2. Shrimp Tacos w/Avocado Aioli

3. Mediterranean Baked Cod

4. Seared Ahi Tuna Steaks w/Oven Roasted Broccoli

5. Tuscan White Fish w/Chickpea Salad

Cilantro Lime Shrimp Skillet

Servings: 4
Time: 30 minutes

- 2 Tbsp avocado oil (divided)
- 1lb raw shrimp, tails removed/deveined
- 4 garlic cloves, minced
- 1 Tbsp Old Bay seasoning
- 1 lime, juiced, zested, divided
- 1 cup brown rice (uncooked)
- 2½ cups chicken broth
- ½ tsp sea salt
- 1 can black beans, rinsed and drained
- 1 can diced tomatoes, not drained
- ¼ cup cilantro, chopped
- ½ tsp cumin
- ¼ tsp coriander

How it's made

1. In a small bowl, toss the shrimp in the Old Bay seasoning to coat all the shrimp.

2. Heat a large skillet on medium-low heat and add 1/2 the avocado oil. Cook the shrimp about 3 minutes on one side, flip, and continue to cook until they are no longer translucent. Remove them from the pan and set aside.

3. In the same skillet, add the chicken broth. Scrape the pan to get all the delicious bits from the shrimp. Now add the uncooked rice and sea salt. Bring to a boil. Lower heat, put on the lid, and cook for 20–25 minutes or until rice is fully cooked. Try not to lift the lid.

4. Add the tomatoes, black beans, cilantro. lime juice, lime zest, cumin, coriander, and shrimp to the cooked rice.

5. Stir and let cook for up to 5 minutes on low. Serve with extra cilantro and lime juice.

Protein: shrimp, black beans
Fiber: black beans
Healthy fat: avocado oil

Notes

Shrimp Tacos w/Avocado Aioli

Servings: 8
Time: 25 minutes

For the Shrimp

- 1lb shrimp (tails off/deveined)
- 1 tsp chili powder
- 1 tsp paprika
- 1 tsp cumin (divided)
- ½ tsp oregano
- ¼ tsp red pepper flakes
- 1 Tbsp lime juice (about 1 lime)
- 3 Tbsp avocado oil
- 1 tsp sea salt (divided)

For the Aioli

- 1 avocado
- ½ cup cilantro
- 1 jalapeno (seeds and veins removed)
- 3 garlic cloves, minced
- 3 Tbsp lime juice
- ½ cup unsweetened coconut yogurt (any non-dairy unflavored yogurt)
- 3 Tbsp avocado oil

For the Slaw

- ½ cup purple cabbage, shredded
- ½ cup green cabbage, shredded
- ½ cup unsweetened coconut yogurt (any non-dairy unflavored yogurt)
- ½ tsp sea salt
- ½ tsp cumin
- A squeeze of lime juice

Taco Add-ons

- 1 avocado, sliced
- Lime wedges
- 8 corn tortillas
- 2 Tbsp cilantro, chopped

How it's made

1. Place shrimp in a bowl with all the seasonings. Stir to coat the shrimp and set it in the fridge to keep cool while you prep the aioli.

2. In a small food processor or high-speed blender, combine one avocado, cilantro, jalapeno, garlic, lime juice, yogurt, avocado oil, and sea salt. Blend well. Add small amounts of water if it's too thick. Set aside.

3. Heat a skillet on medium with some avocado oil or non-stick cooking spray. Sauté your shrimp for 2–3 minutes on each side until no longer pink. Set aside.

4. In a small bowl, combine the cabbage, the yogurt, a little cumin, sea salt, and a few dashes of lime juice. Mix well for a slaw topping.

5. Assemble your tacos by placing the slaw in the bottom, then the shrimp, and drizzle with aioli sauce. Garnish with cilantro, lime, and sliced avocado.

Protein: shrimp
Fiber: cabbage, avocado
Healthy fat: avocado oil, avocado

Notes

Mediterranean Baked Cod

Servings: 2
Time: 30 minutes

- 1 cup quinoa, uncooked
- 1½ cups water
- ⅓ cup avocado oil
- 2 cod fillets
- ½ tsp sea salt
- ¼ tsp black pepper
- ½ tsp red pepper flakes
- 4 garlic cloves, thinly sliced
- 1½ cups cherry tomatoes
- 1 Tbsp capers
- ¼ cup pitted Kalamata olives
- ¼ cup pickled banana peppers, sliced
- 2 Tbsp sun-dried tomatoes, sliced or chopped
- 2 tsp thyme

How it's made

1. Preheat the oven to 400°F (204°C). Add avocado oil to a baking dish and place in oven for 6–8 minutes.

2. Rinse your quinoa. Add 1½ cups of water to a pot and add in your quinoa. Bring to a boil. As soon as it bubbles, reduce the heat to low, cover, and cook for 8 minutes (or until all the water is evaporated). Take the lid off, fluff it with a fork, and set aside.

3. While the oil heats, rinse and pat dry your cod fillets and sprinkle with red pepper flakes, sea salt, and black pepper. Set aside.

4. Remove the baking dish and immediately add the sliced garlic, thyme, tomatoes, olives, peppers, sun-dried tomatoes, and capers. Now nestle the cod fillets in between all the goodies in the baking dish. Spoon some of the mixture over the fillets. If you want super moist fish, cover it with foil. Bake for 15–20 minutes or until fish is 145°F (63°C).

5. Place quinoa on individual plates. Add the cod fillets to the plates and top the fish with all the goodies from the baking dish. Enjoy!

Protein: cod, quinoa
Healthy fat: avocado oil

Tip

This dish pairs really well with steamed asparagus.

If you want my homemade recipe for pickled banana peppers, head to the recipes page on my website: shelleycanhelp.com/recipes

Notes

Seared Ahi Tuna Steaks w/Oven-Roasted Broccoli

Servings: 2
Time: 20 minutes

For the Tuna

- 1lb Ahi tuna (2 steaks)
- 3 Tbsp sesame seeds
- 2 Tbsp sesame oil
- 1 tsp sea salt
- 1 tsp black pepper

For the Broccoli

- 2 cups broccoli (cut into florets)
- 1 Tbsp avocado oil
- 1 Tbsp lemon juice
- 2 garlic cloves, minced
- ½ tsp sea salt
- ¼ tsp black pepper

How it's made

1. Set your tuna steaks out on the counter so they get close to room temperature. I usually let them rest for 30–40 minutes.

2. Preheat the oven to 400°F (204°C). In a bowl mix the avocado oil, lemon juice, garlic, sea salt, and black pepper. Toss the broccoli florets around in the mixture and evenly spread them on a baking sheet lined with parchment paper. Bake for 10 minutes. Take them out, give them a toss, and cook for another 2–3 minutes.

3. In a small mixing bowl, whisk together the tamari, sesame oil, garlic powder, maple syrup, rice vinegar, and red pepper flakes. Set aside.

4. Place your sesame seeds on a plate (I like to use both black and white seeds). Take your tuna steaks and spray avocado oil cooking spray on both sides. Now dredge your steaks in the sesame seeds on all sides and sprinkle them with a little sea salt.

5. Heat a skillet (I prefer a cast-iron skillet for this recipe) on medium-high. Drizzle some sesame oil and avocado oil in the pan and let it get hot.

6. Place your steaks in the skillet and cook for about 90 seconds. Turn them over and cook for another 90 seconds to 2 minutes. You want the center to still be pink.

7. Place your tuna steaks on your serving plates over the cooked broccoli. Take your tamari mixture, give it one more good whisk, and place it in a small serving bowl for dipping your tuna. Enjoy!

Protein: tuna, sesame seeds
Fiber: broccoli
Healthy fat: oils

Notes

Tuscan White Fish w/Chickpea Salad

Servings: 4
Time: 30 minutes

- 2 Tbsp avocado oil (divided)
- ½ tsp red pepper flakes
- 1 tsp oregano
- 1 leek, only the white part, diced
- 1 pint cherry tomatoes, cut in half
- 3 garlic cloves, minced
- 1 cup asparagus (cut into bite-sized pieces)
- ¼ cup white cooking wine
- 2 Tbsp basil leaves (chopped)
- 2 Tbsp lemon juice
- ¼ tsp lemon zest (about half a lemon)
- 1 Tbsp capers
- 4 cod fillets
- ½ tsp sea salt
- ½ tsp black pepper
- 1 can chickpeas, rinsed, drained
- ½ cucumber, diced
- ¼ cup pitted Kalamata olives
- 2 Tbsp fresh dill, chopped
- ¼ cup extra-virgin olive oil
- ¼ cup balsamic vinegar
- ¼ tsp garlic powder
- ⅛ tsp black pepper (pinch)

How it's made

1. First, rinse, pat dry, and sprinkle the cod with sea salt and black pepper. Set aside.

2. Heat a large skillet on low and add half the avocado oil. Heat for 1 minute. Add the red pepper flakes and oregano, and heat for 30 seconds. Give them a quick toss around the pan to coat them with the oil.

3. Add the leeks and cook for 1–2 minutes or until they become soft.

4. Add the cherry tomatoes and stir. Cover and let them "blister" for 10–12 minutes.

5. Remove the lid and add in the asparagus and wine. Give everything a stir. If you have anything sticking to the pan, now is the time to give the pan a good scrape with a wooden spoon or rubber spatula.

6. After a minute or so, add in the basil, lemon juice, lemon zest, and capers. Cook on low for 5 minutes or so. Watch the asparagus. You want to make sure it stays bright green. If it starts turning a dull color, it's overcooked.

7. Remove the solids from the pan (leaving all the yummy juices) and place them in a bowl. Now add your cod fillets to the sauce, coat them with the sauce, cover and cook for 2 minutes. Flip them and cook until very tender (about 3–4 minutes total).

8. While the cod is cooking, in a bowl add the chickpeas, cucumber, remaining tomatoes, red onion, kalamata olives, and dill. Toss really well. Add the extra-virgin olive oil, balsamic vinegar, garlic powder, and black pepper to a bowl or measuring cup and whisk until combined. Pour over the salad mixture.

9. Add all the sauteed veggies back to the pan with the cod, turn off the heat, and put the lid on. Let it just sit and steam for a minute or so then serve with your chickpea salad.

Protein: cod
Fiber: leeks, asparagus
Healthy fat: avocado oil

Tip

Buy wild-caught seafood. It is the best sourced fish you can buy. Farm-raised fish and shellfish are often fed growth hormones, a poor diet, and are stressed because they aren't in their natural environment.

Notes

Behind The Scenes

In 2017, a month before I registered for my first nutrition school, I decided we needed a puppy. We had lost one of our dogs to a tragic accident when we lived in Florida. So, a year later, I felt the need to fill that hole in our family. I didn't tell my husband because he had warned me NOT to get any more dogs. But his mom told me "Don't tell Neil you are getting a puppy. When you bring her home, he will fall in love."

So, I did it. I drove to central Oklahoma from our home outside Dallas to pick up Millie Sue. I brought her home and my husband was so mad at me! He didn't say much to me for about forty-eight hours, but he fell in love with Millie very quickly.

There I was, one month later, diving into nutrition school. Once completing each lesson, I would then go to the store, buy some ingredients, and try out new recipes. I was on a mission. I had those racing horse blinders on, and I wasn't looking back. We were going to get healthy, and we were going to do it naturally...with food.

As I made these recipes, I had this adorable little black puppy at my feet. She quickly learned that when she heard the sound of the knife on the cutting board, that it was her cue for "snacks." You see, I am a very messy cook, so I drop food on the floor, spill food on my clothes, and even drop scraps on Millie's head. She loved it all! She never left my side through my year studying with IIN.

I began cooking three meals (and two snacks) a day five to six days a week. Neil got to the point where he didn't want to eat out anymore while he was working. He relied on me (and fully trusted me) to create healthy meals for him. It was our thing. It became second nature. Funny how things happen. Just six months prior, I was feeling hopeless and useless. Now, I was healing us. When we go through the valleys, we don't see the good in them. We survive. We put one foot in front of the other; we take one minute at a time. Each minute, each day I had my focus on food and health.

By 2019, when I attended The Academy of Culinary Nutrition, Millie was a sous chef pro! She would come running to the kitchen just when she heard the cutting board coming out of the drawer. I didn't realize it at the time, but Millie really helped me get through school. She kept me company, ate my mistakes (all the yummy vegetable scraps) and became my dedicated audience.

I've never seen a dog that loves vegetables and fruits quite as much as Millie does. Now don't panic. I have done my homework and I am very clear on what dogs can't eat. And honestly, if I accidently drop one, she doesn't even want it. Funny how instinctual dogs are with what they know they can't have. I wish humans could be better at that.

Unfortunately, we have big box companies that manufacture terrible "food" that's addicting so that we buy more of it. If I could have one wish come true for society as a whole, it would be that the FDA would actually really care about our health and make products and medications that don't slowly kill us. Everyone has a pipe dream, right?

It's 2022, and I have spent the entire year creating recipes for this cookbook. That means rolling up my sleeves and creating recipes that are somewhat simple, anti-inflammatory, and delicious. Perfecting these recipes meant I made most of them two to four times. My friends and family will tell you I put a TON of pressure on myself, so I knew when it came to writing my first cookbook, it was going to consume me. And it has. I can't take full credit for this book as there are a lot of people that I'm grateful for, but the first one I am going to thank is Millie Sue. She kept me company, cleaned up my messes, and was always by my side with every recipe...every day this year.

Mix-n-Match

You pick the protein
and
You pick the vegetable

The next sixteen recipes are a fun little idea I had when creating this cookbook. Sometimes we don't need huge meals. Sometimes we need quick ideas that aren't boring. This section will give you over sixty meal ideas!

You just take one of the eight protein recipes and pair it with one of the vegetable recipes. Have fun with these recipes. I sure had fun creating them!

Proteins

1. Baked Chicken Thighs
2. Stuffed Chicken Breasts
3. Veggie Meat(less) Balls
4. Turkey Veggie Bites
5. Versatile Turkey Meatballs w/Quinoa
6. Almond-crusted Salmon w/Honey Dijon
7. Coconut Shrimp

Baked Chicken Thighs

Servings: 4
Time: 30 minutes

- 1 red bell pepper, cut into chunks, seeds removed
- 1 jalapeno, cut into chunks, seeds removed
- ¼ cup cilantro, chopped
- 1 tsp paprika
- 2 Tbsp lemon juice
- 3 garlic cloves, minced
- ½ tsp raw honey
- 2 Tbsp avocado oil, divided
- ½ tsp sea salt, divided
- 1lb boneless chicken thighs with skin

How it's made

1. In a food processor or blender, add bell pepper, jalapeno, cilantro, paprika, lemon juice, garlic, raw honey, half of the avocado oil, and half of the sea salt. Blend until smooth.

2. In a large bowl, add the chicken thighs along with the sauce and let it marinate on the counter for 20–30 minutes.

3. Preheat the oven to 425°F (218°C) and line a baking sheet with parchment paper. Add the chicken to the pan. Place in the oven and bake for 20 minutes. Broil for an additional 4–5 minutes. Make sure the internal temperature is 165°.

4. Remove from the oven and let it cool slightly. Top with additional cilantro if desired and enjoy!

Protein: chicken
Healthy fat: avocado oil

Pairs well with:
Roasted Brussels Sprouts with a Kick

Notes

Stuffed Chicken Breasts

Servings: 4
Time: 35 minutes

- 1lb chicken breast, boneless
- 2 Tbsp avocado oil, divided
- 2 cups baby spinach, finely chopped
- ¼ cup vegan Parmesan
- 1 tsp sea salt, divided
- 3 Tbsp nutritional yeast
- 1 Tbsp ghee, melted
- ¼ cup almonds, chopped
- 2 garlic cloves

How it's made

1. Preheat the oven to 425°F (218°C).

2. Make a slice lengthwise in each chicken breast to create a deep pocket. Coat well with half the oil and set aside.

3. In a food processor or chopper, blend together the spinach, vegan Parmesan, nutritional yeast, melted ghee, almonds, garlic and half the sea salt until well combined. Stuff the mixture into each chicken breast. Transfer chicken to baking dish. Sprinkle with sea salt and bake for 15–20 minutes or until chicken is 165°.

4. Remove the chicken from the oven and serve. Enjoy!

Protein: chicken, nutritional yeast, almonds
Fiber: spinach
Healthy fat: ghee, avocado oil

Tips

Nutritional yeast isn't just for vegans. It really adds a deeper level of flavor to many dishes, and it's loaded with antioxidants and has protein. It's a great substitute for adding cheese to your recipes, but it also has a lot of nutritional value.

Reason for the nuts: I don't use breadcrumbs in my recipes because gluten is inflammatory, and they don't have any nutritional value. So, for any recipe that calls for breadcrumbs, I just crush up nuts. Almonds and cashews are my go-to, but any nut will work beautifully!

Pairs well with:
Dairy-free Pesto and
Italian Stuffed Portobellos

Notes

Veggie Meat(less) Balls

Servings: 6
Time: 25 minutes

- ½ cup quinoa, cooked
- 1 can black beans, rinsed/drained
- 1 Tbsp ground flax seed
- ¼ cup almonds
- ¼ cup sunflower seeds
- ½ cup oats
- 1 can fire-roasted diced tomatoes, drained (or Rotel)
- 2 Tbsp tomato paste
- ½ yellow onion, diced
- 2 garlic cloves, minced
- 2 Tbsp chia seeds
- 1 Tbsp nutritional yeast
- 2 tsp onion powder
- 2 tsp garlic powder
- 1 Tbsp oregano
- ½ tsp paprika
- ¼ tsp red pepper flakes
- 1 tsp cumin
- 1 tsp sea salt
- ½ tsp black pepper
- 1 Tbsp lemon juice
- ½ cup baby spinach

How it's made

1. Heat oven to 375°F (190°C) and line a baking sheet with parchment paper.

2. First, place the almonds and sunflower seeds in a food processor or high-speed blender. Grind them up. Now add everything else to the food processor and blend. Once the mixture is well blended, form balls (I use a medium-sized melon baller) and place on a parchment-lined baking sheet.

3. Bake them for 13–15 minutes or until cooked through. Serve with your favorite marinara sauce OR use one of my homemade sauce recipes. Enjoy!

Protein: quinoa, almonds, sunflower seeds, chia seeds, nutritional yeast, black beans
Fiber: spinach, black beans, oats
Healthy fat: almonds

Pairs well with:
Cabbage Steaks and Tahini Dipping Sauce

I'm really proud of these meat(less) balls. They have so much flavor. I promise you won't miss the meat!

Notes

Turkey Veggie Bites

Servings: 4
Time: 25 minutes

- 1lb extra-lean ground turkey
- 1 medium carrot, peeled and grated
- 1 beet, peeled and grated
- 1 Tbsp sea salt
- ½ tsp dried thyme
- 1 Tbsp Dijon mustard
- 1 Tbsp mayonnaise
- 1 tsp black pepper
- 2 garlic cloves, minced
- ½ tsp onion powder
- 1 tsp ground flax seed
- 1 Tbsp parsley, chopped
- 1 Tbsp Worcestershire sauce

How it's made

1. Preheat the oven to 400°F (200°C) and line a baking sheet with parchment paper.

2. In a large mixing bowl, use your hands or a spatula and combine all the ingredients.

3. I use a melon baller to create even balls, but you can just pinch off a heaping tablespoon of the mixture and roll in a ball. Place on the parchment-lined baking sheet and mash down to form a small patty. Repeat with the rest of the turkey mixture. Heat for 12–14 minutes or until cooked through.

4. Transfer to a plate lined with a paper towel to remove all excess moisture. Enjoy!

Protein: turkey, ground flax
Fiber: beet, carrot, ground flax

Pairs well with:
Creamy Zucchini and Magic Green Sauce

Notes

Versatile Turkey Meatballs w/Quinoa

Servings: 4
Time: 35 minutes

- ½ cup quinoa, uncooked
- ¾ cup water
- 1 egg
- 1lb extra-lean ground turkey
- ½ cup cilantro, chopped
- 1 tsp fresh ginger, minced
- 2 tsp fish sauce
- 1 tsp coconut sugar
- ½ lime, juice and zest
- ½ cup almonds, finely chopped
- 3 Tbsp brown rice flour (can also use oat flour)

How it's made

1. Rinse your quinoa for 20 seconds in a fine mesh colander. Place the quinoa and water in a saucepan over medium-high heat and bring to a boil. Once boiling, cover and reduce heat to very low. Let it simmer for 6–8 minutes. All the water should be evaporated. Remove from heat, fluff with a fork and set aside.

2. Preheat the oven to 400°F (204°C) and line a baking sheet with parchment paper.

3. In a large bowl, add the egg and beat with a fork. To the same bowl, add the turkey, cilantro, ginger, fish sauce, coconut sugar, lime juice, ground almonds, zest, and mix well. Add the quinoa and the rice flour and mix it again.

4. Roll the chicken mixture into balls slightly bigger than a golf ball. Place them on the baking sheet and bake for 12–15 minutes. Make sure the internal temperature is 165°F (75°C). Remove, serve, and enjoy!

Protein: quinoa, turkey, nuts, egg

Tips

Any gluten-free flour will work, or you can also chop quick oats for added texture.

This recipe is also really good in soups. Just make your meatballs bite-sized.

Pairs well with:

Citrus & Sesame Bok Choy and Tahini Dipping Sauce

Notes

Almond Crusted Salmon w/Honey Dijon

Servings: 4
Time: 25 minutes

- 2lbs salmon fillets (4 fillets)
- ⅓ cup almonds, finely chopped
- 2 Tbsp nutritional yeast
- 3 garlic cloves, minced
- 1 Tbsp parsley, chopped
- 1 tsp thyme, finely chopped
- 1 stalk green onions, finely chopped
- ½ tsp sea salt
- ¼ tsp black pepper
- 3 Tbsp ghee, melted, (can use avocado oil)
- 1 lemon, thinly sliced (optional garnish)
- 2 Tbsp raw honey
- ¼ cup Dijon mustard

How it's made

1. In a small bowl, combine the ground almonds, nutritional yeast, garlic, herbs, sea salt, and black pepper. Now add in your melted ghee or avocado oil and mix until well combined.

2. Spread the herb mixture over each salmon fillet and press down to help bind it. Top each fillet with lemon slices and broil for 6-7 minutes.

3. In a measuring cup, mix the honey and Dijon mustard. Set aside.

4. Once salmon is cooked, let it cool for 1 minute and remove the skin. You can pour the honey Dijon over the fillets, or you can serve it as a dipping sauce.

Protein: salmon, almonds, nutritional yeast
Healthy fat: ghee, almonds

Pairs well with: *Roasted Broccoli*

Notes

Coconut Shrimp

Servings: 2
Time: 20 minutes

- 2 Tbsp tapioca flour
- 2 Tbsp coconut flour
- ⅓ cup unsweetened shredded coconut
- 1 lime (zested)
- ¼ cup canned full fat coconut milk
- 8 ozs shrimp, peeled, deveined, tail attached
- 1½ tsp coconut oil
- ¼ cup cilantro, finely chopped (for garnish)

How it's made

1. On a small plate or bowl, add the tapioca flour. On a separate plate add the coconut flour, shredded coconut, and lime zest. Mix well to combine. In a small bowl, add the coconut milk.

2. One by one, dip the shrimp in the tapioca flour and shake off any excess. Then dip in the coconut milk, shaking off any excess. Then dip in the shredded coconut mixture. Place on a plate and repeat until all the shrimp are done.

3. Heat a skillet over medium heat and add the coconut oil. Add each shrimp to the pan and cook for 3–4 minutes per side. Divide onto plates and top with cilantro. Enjoy!

Protein: shrimp
Healthy fat: coconut milk, coconut oil

Pairs well with: *Sweet & Spicy Cauliflower*

Notes

Vegetable Sides

1. Roasted Brussels Sprouts with a Kick
2. Italian Stuffed Portobellos
3. Citrus & Sesame Bok Choy
4. Spicy Cauliflower Steaks
5. Roasted Broccoli
6. Cabbage Steaks
7. Creamy Zucchini
8. Sweet & Spicy Cauliflower

Roasted Brussels Sprouts with a Kick

Servings: 4
Time: 30 minutes

For the Brussels Sprouts

- 4 cups Brussels sprouts (halved, trimmed)
- 2 tsp avocado oil
- ½ tsp sea salt
- ¼ tsp black pepper

For the Sauce

- ½ cup almond butter
- 1 garlic clove, minced
- Juice of 1 lime
- 2 tsp tamari
- ½ tsp sriracha
- 1 Tbsp water

Add-ons

- ¼ cup cilantro, chopped
- 2 Tbsp slivered almonds, crushed

How it's made

1. Preheat the oven to 425°F (220°C) and line a baking sheet with parchment paper.

2. In a medium-sized bowl, add the Brussels sprouts and avocado oil. Season with salt and pepper to taste and toss well. Transfer to the baking sheet and place in the oven. Bake for 15–17 minutes until crispy and browned.

3. Meanwhile, in a small bowl, add the almond butter, garlic, lime juice, tamari, sriracha, and water. Whisk to combine.

4. When ready to serve, drizzle the sauce on top of the roasted Brussels sprouts and top with cilantro and slivered almonds. Enjoy!

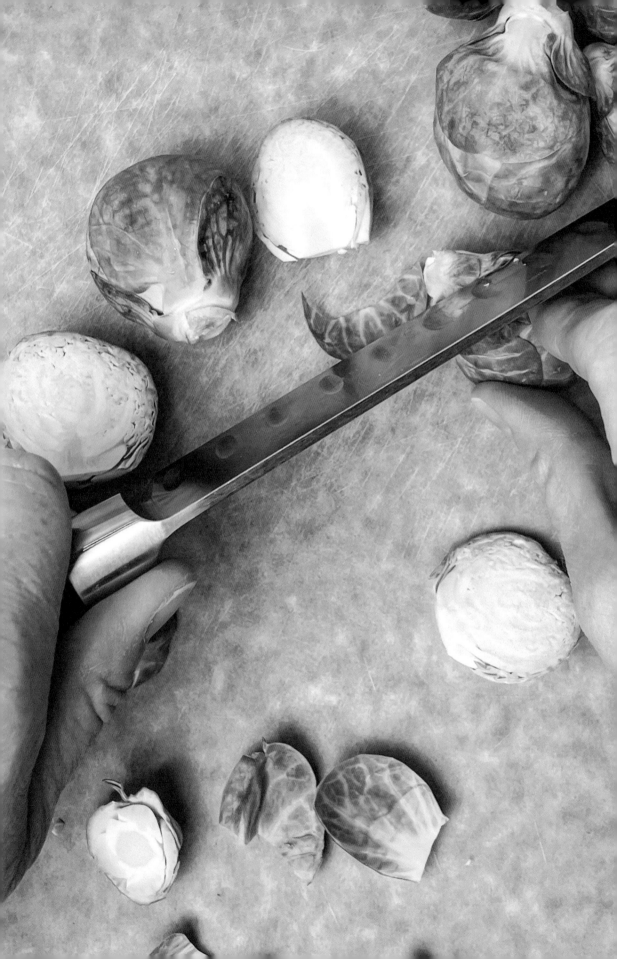

Protein: almond butter
Fiber: Brussels sprouts
Healthy fat: avocado oil

Pairs well with:

These Brussels sprouts are also delicious with Magic Green Sauce

Notes

Italian Stuffed Portobellos

Servings: 2
Time: 20 minutes

- 2 large Portobello mushrooms
- 2 Tbsp avocado oil (divided)
- 2 leeks (the white part), thinly sliced
- 1 cup organic diced tomatoes
- ½ cup tomato sauce (or marinara)
- 2 garlic cloves, minced
- 1 tsp oregano
- ½ cup quinoa, cooked
- ½ cup baby spinach, chopped
- 1 tsp sea salt
- ½ tsp black pepper
- 1 Tbsp nutritional yeast
- 2 Tbsp vegan Parmesan (shredded – optional)
- 4 basil leaves, chopped

How it's made

1. Heat oven to 350°F (176°C). Scrape out the center of the mushrooms, brush them with half the avocado oil (both sides) place them (scooped side up) in a baking pan, and cook for 5–7 minutes.

2. While they cook, heat a skillet on low and add some avocado oil. Simmer the garlic for one minute. Add the leeks and sauté for 3-4 minutes until they are soft. Add in the tomatoes and tomato sauce (I prefer marinara) and all the seasonings along with the nutritional yeast. Simmer for 5-10 minutes, letting all those flavors join together.

3. Turn the heat off the vegetable mixture and stir in the chopped spinach.

4. Stuff the mushroom caps with the vegetable filling. You can now add some vegan shredded Parmesan if you choose. Bake for 10–12 minutes. Enjoy!

Protein: quinoa, nutritional yeast
Fiber: spinach
Healthy fat: avocado oil

Tips

If you don't have vegan Parmesan, you can sprinkle some nutritional yeast in with the vegetables before you assemble the mushrooms to add some richness/cheesy flavors.

Wash your leeks really well. They hide quite a bit of dirt between the layers.

My favorite marinara sauces that have quality ingredients are Rao's and Otamot.

Fun Fact

Mushrooms are what they call an immune stabilizer. *If your immune system is running low, they will help to boost it. If you have an overactive immune system (auto-immune disease), mushrooms will work to calm it down. Isn't that amazing?!*

Notes

Citrus & Sesame Bok Choy

Servings: 4
Time: 15 minutes

For the Bok Choy

- 1 tsp sesame oil
- ½ yellow onion, chopped
- 1 garlic clove, minced
- 1 tsp ginger, finely grated
- 6 cups bok choy

For the Sauce

- 1 lemon, juiced and zested
- 1 Tbsp tamari (or coconut aminos)
- 2 tsp raw honey
- ⅛ tsp sea salt

Garnish

- ½ tsp sesame seeds

How it's made

1. Juice your lemon and zest about half of it.

2. Cut leaves off the bok choy, chop them, and set them aside. Now chop the stalks. Keep them separate.

3. In a small mixing bowl, whisk together lemon juice, lemon zest, tamari, honey, and sea salt. Set aside.

4. Heat the sesame oil in a large non-stick pan over medium-low heat. Add the onion and sauté until translucent. Lower the heat and add in the garlic and ginger. Sauté for up to 1 minute. Don't burn it. Add in the chopped bok choy (not the leaves yet) and sauté for 4–6 minutes or until crisp but cooked.

5. Add the lemon juice mixture to the pan, stir to combine with the bok choy, and cook for another minute. Now add in the chopped bok choy leaves. Season with additional salt if needed. Turn off the heat. Top with sesame seeds. Enjoy!

Protein: sesame seeds
Fiber: bok choy
Healthy fat: sesame oil
Anti-inflammatory: honey, bok choy

Tip

Bok choy is one of those forgotten vegetables at all the grocery stores. But it shouldn't be neglected because it's so delicious, versatile, and loaded with anti-inflammatory properties.

Notes

Spicy Cauliflower Steaks

Servings: 6
Time: 30 minutes

- 1 head cauliflower
- ¼ cup extra-virgin olive oil
- 2 Tbsp lemon juice (juice of one lemon)
- 2 garlic cloves, minced
- 1 tsp sea salt
- ½ tsp smoked paprika
- ¼ tsp chili powder
- 1 tsp coconut sugar
- ⅛ tsp black pepper (pinch)
- 2 Tbsp cilantro, chopped (divided)

How it's made

1. Preheat the oven to 425°F (218°C). Set the cauliflower heads upright and cut them into three pieces (so two vertical cuts in each head). It's good to keep the stem attached. It helps them stay together.

2. In a measuring cup, whisk together the oil, lemon, garlic, sea salt, smoked paprika, coconut sugar, chili powder, pepper, and half the cilantro.

3. Heat an oven-safe shallow sauté pan over medium-low heat. You will need two pans. Pour the oil mixture equally into the two pans and heat for 2–3 minutes. Lay the cauliflower slices down in the oil mixture and sauté until golden brown (5–7 minutes). Flip them and sauté/brown the other side of each cauliflower steak.

4. Place the (oven safe) sauté pans with the cauliflower steaks in them in the oven and bake for 20–25 minutes or until fork tender. To serve, top them with the remaining cilantro.

Fiber: cauliflower
Healthy fat: extra-virgin olive oil

Notes

Roasted Broccoli

Servings: 4
Time: 15 minutes

- 4 cups broccoli (2 large heads)
- 2 Tbsp avocado oil
- ½ tsp garlic powder
- 1 Tbsp nutritional yeast
- ½ tsp sea salt
- ¼ tsp black pepper

How it's made

1. Preheat the oven to 425°F (218°C). Wash the broccoli and make sure it's completely dry. This will help the broccoli stay crispy. Cut into bite-sized florets and place them in a bowl. Toss the oil around in the bowl with the florets to get good coverage on all pieces.

2. In a small bowl, combine the spices/ seasonings and sprinkle them in the bowl with the broccoli. Give the broccoli a very good toss to coat all of it.

3. Spread them out (try not to let them touch each other so they all cook evenly) on a parchment-lined baking sheet and cook for 10–12 minutes.

Protein: nutritional yeast
Fiber: broccoli
Healthy fat: avocado oil

Notes

Cabbage Steaks

Servings: 4
Time: 25 minutes

- 1 head green cabbage (sliced into 1½-inch pieces)
- 1 Tbsp avocado oil
- 1 tsp sea salt
- 1 tsp black pepper

For the Sauce

- 2 Tbsp red wine vinegar
- 1 Tbsp Dijon mustard
- 1 Tbsp whole grain mustard
- 3 Tbsp honey
- 2 garlic cloves, minced

Add-ons

- ¼ cup slivered almonds
- 2 Tbsp parsley (chopped)

How it's made

1. Preheat oven to 400°F (204°C). Place your cabbage slices on a parchment-lined baking sheet. Rub avocado oil on each piece and sprinkle with sea salt and black pepper. Bake for 20–25 minutes or until they start to get brown edges.

2. While the cabbage cooks, toast your slivered almonds in a small sauté pan over low heat (no oil) until they begin to brown. Remove from heat and set aside.

3. To make the dressing, add the vinegar, both mustards, honey, and garlic to a bowl and whisk until well combined.

4. Remove cabbage from the oven. Drizzle with the dressing and top with toasted almonds and fresh parsley. Enjoy!

Protein: almonds
Fiber: cabbage
Healthy fat: avocado oil

Notes

Creamy Zucchini

Servings: 4
Time: 30 minutes

For the Zucchini

- 2 large zucchini (diced large)
- 2 Tbsp extra-virgin olive oil
- ½ tsp sea salt
- 2 tsp paprika

For the Sauce

- 1 cup full-fat canned coconut milk
- 2 Tbsp tomato paste
- 3 garlic cloves, minced
- ¼ cup parsley, finely chopped
- ¼ cup basil leaves, finely chopped
- ½ cup roasted red peppers (see my homemade recipe on page 203)
- ⅛ tsp red pepper flakes
- ¼ tsp arrowroot powder
- ½ tsp water
- 2 stalks green onions, diced
- ¼ cup vegan Parmesan (see my homemade recipe)

How it's made

1. Preheat the oven to 400°F (218°C) and line a baking sheet with parchment paper or a silicone mat. Dice the zucchini into medium-sized cubes and place in a bowl. Toss with olive oil, sea salt, and paprika. Spread on the baking sheet and bake for 15–20 minutes.

2. While they cook, let's make the sauce. Heat a sauté pan on low. Low is key. Pour in the coconut milk and add the tomato paste, garlic, parsley, basil, roasted peppers, and red pepper flakes. Whisk often so nothing sticks or burns.

3. Let it cook on low for 5–10 minutes. You should see small simmer bubbles.

4. When the zucchini is cooked, add it to the sauce and simmer for another 1–2 minutes. If the sauce isn't thick enough, you can then add a slurry. In a small bowl, take the arrowroot powder and whisk it in with the water to form a slurry. Add that mixture to the sauce and stir.

5. Put zucchini in individual serving bowls and top with diced green onions and vegan Parmesan. Enjoy!

Fiber: zucchini
Healthy fat: coconut milk, extra-virgin olive oil

Notes

Sweet & Spicy Cauliflower

Servings: 4
Time: 25 minutes

For the Cauliflower

- 1 head cauliflower (large)
- 1 tsp avocado oil
- ½ tsp garlic powder
- 1 tsp sea salt
- ½ tsp black pepper
- ½ cup raw honey
- 2 garlic cloves, minced
- ¼ cup tamari
- 1 Tbsp sriracha
- 1 Tbsp hoisin sauce (or can use more honey)
- ½ tsp red pepper flakes
- ½ tsp arrowroot powder

Add-ons

- 2 stalks green onions, diced
- 1 tsp sesame seeds (I prefer black)

How it's made

1. Preheat the oven to 400°F (204°C) and line a baking sheet with parchment paper.

2. Cut up the cauliflower into bite-sized florets and put them in a bowl. Add in the avocado oil, garlic powder, sea salt, and black pepper. Give it a good toss and place the seasoned florets on the baking sheet. Bake for 20 minutes or when they start to turn brown on the tips.

3. While the cauliflower cooks, heat a small saucepan over low heat, and all the sauce ingredients (honey-arrowroot powder). Continually whisk until the sauce just begins to bubble and get thick. Take the saucepan off the heat and set it aside.

4. When you take the cauliflower out of the oven, let it sit for 1–2 minutes to cool slightly. Place the cauliflower in a serving bowl and toss it with the sauce. Top with diced green onion and black sesame seeds. White sesame seeds are fine too. I just love the pretty contrast of the black against the cauliflower. Enjoy!

Fiber: cauliflower
Healthy fat: avocado oil

Notes

Condiments

Store-bought condiments are one of the most inflammatory foods on the shelves today. Convenient? Of course. But be careful! Most of them are full of junk. In this section, I'll show you how quick it is to whip up some of your own delicious sauces and more!

1. Dairy-free Pesto

2. Tahini Dipping Sauce

3. Magic Green Sauce

4. Dairy-free Ranch Dressing

5. Taco Seasoning

6. Parmesan (Non-Cheesy) Powder

7. Homemade Roasted Peppers

Dairy-free Pesto

Servings: 4
Time: 20 minutes

- ½ cup cashews
- 2 garlic cloves
- 3 Tbsp pine nuts
- 2 Tbsp nutritional yeast
- ¼ cup extra-virgin olive oil (may need more)
- 1 Tbsp lemon juice
- ½ cup basil leaves (packed)
- 1 cup baby spinach (can also use kale)
- ¼ cup water (may need more)
- 1 tsp sea salt
- 1 tsp black pepper

How it's made

1. First, soak your cashews in hot water for at least 20 minutes. Longer is always better so they will be super soft. I like to cover them to help trap the steam.

2. Rinse and drain the cashews and place them in a high-speed blender. Next, add lemon juice, garlic, pine nuts, nutritional yeast, a little water, and part of the olive oil. Give it all a good blend.

3. Now add the leaves of basil and kale and/or spinach. Feel free to get creative on this step. Mix up your greens, add more basil. It's up to you and your taste buds. Remember, these are all healthy ingredients. Have fun with them!

4. It's time to thin it out. Be sure to taste it first. Add water, lemon juice, or olive oil slowly until the pesto has the consistency you like. I tend to like mine a little thinner so that it adheres to pasta easily.

5. Add salt and pepper to your taste and you are done. You can store this for up to five days in the fridge or you can put it in ice cube trays and freeze it.

Protein: cashews, pine nuts
Fiber: all the greens
Healthy fat: extra-virgin olive oil, pine nuts

Notes

Tahini Dipping Sauce

Servings: 4
Time: 5 minutes

- ¼ cup tahini
- 3 garlic cloves, minced
- ¼ cup extra-virgin olive oil
- 2 Tbsp apple cider vinegar
- 2 Tbsp lemon juice
- 2 Tbsp tamari
- 1 Tbsp maple syrup
- ½ tsp sea salt

How it's made

1. Whisk everything together and enjoy! Don't forget to taste it as you mix it and add any extra of what you think it needs for YOUR liking.

Protein: tahini
Healthy fat: extra-virgin olive oil

Notes

Magic Green Sauce

Servings: 4
Time: 5 minutes

- 2 avocadoes
- ¼ cup lime juice
- 3 garlic cloves
- ¼ cup cilantro roughly chopped
- ¼ tsp cumin
- ¼ tsp sea salt

- ⅛ tsp black pepper
- 2 Tbsp unsweetened coconut yogurt (or any dairy-free option)
- 1 Tbsp extra-virgin olive oil (may need a little more)

How it's made

1. Place everything in a blender except the extra-virgin olive oil. Once well combined, add in the EVOO and blend until smooth.

Healthy fat: avocado, extra-virgin olive oil

Tip

I use this sauce as a dip, a spread on a sandwich or wrap, and as a dressing. To make it a dressing, just thin it out with water.

Notes

Dairy-free Ranch Dressing

Servings: 8
Time: 5 minutes

- ½ cup cashews (soaked in hot water)
- 1 cup organic coconut milk (canned, full fat, refrigerated overnight)
- ¼ cup avocado oil
- 1 Tbsp apple cider vinegar
- 1 stalk green onion, chopped
- ½ tsp onion powder
- 1 tsp sea salt
- 1 tsp fresh dill, chopped
- 1 Tbsp parsley, chopped
- ¼ tsp garlic powder
- 1 Tbsp lemon juice

How it's made

1. Place your cashews in hot water and soak them for at least 20 minutes.

2. Drain and rinse cashews and add all ingredients to a high-speed blender and mix until smooth. Refrigerate until ready to serve.

Protein: cashews
Healthy fat: avocado oil

Tip

This ever-so-popular condiment is loaded with refined oils and horrible ingredients. So, making your own is a much healthier option.

Unlike the store-bought ranch dressing, this recipe will be vibrant green in color due to the fresh herbs. This is a good thing! Your ranch dressing SHOULD be green, not white.

Notes

Taco Seasoning

Servings: 4
Time: 5 minutes

- 1 tsp chili powder
- 1 tsp cumin
- ½ tsp coriander
- ½ tsp black pepper
- ½ tsp paprika

- ½ tsp arrowroot powder (or tapioca flour)
- ½ tsp onion powder
- ¼ tsp garlic powder
- ¼ tsp oregano
- ¼ tsp cayenne pepper

How it's made

1. Mix all the spices together and enjoy!

Tip

Most pre-made taco seasonings at the store have unsafe ingredients like MSG. Making your own is easy, quick, and delicious!

Notes

Roasted Red Peppers

Servings: 2 x 8 oz Mason jars
Time: 25 minutes

- 2 red bell peppers
- 2 yellow bell peppers
- 2 orange bell peppers

- 2 cups distilled vinegar
- 3 Tbsp sea salt
- 2 Tbsp extra-virgin olive oil

How it's made

1. Preheat the oven to 400°F (204°C) and line a baking sheet with parchment paper. Remove the tops of the peppers along with the seeds and membranes (the white part). Cut them in half.

2. Place the peppers cut side down on the baking sheet and roast for 20 minutes. Flip them and roast for 15 more minutes.

3. Remove them from the oven, place them all in a bowl and cover them for 15 minutes. The steam will loosen the skin. After 15 minutes, remove the outer skin from all the pepper halves and slice them into strips.

4. Place them in a bowl and cover them with distilled vinegar. Give them a good toss. You just want to cover them. Remove the peppers and place them in a separate bowl (saving the vinegar). Now add salt to the vinegar and stir it.

5. Salt the peppers and toss them around in the bowl. Salt again and toss. Place peppers in 8 oz Mason jars (you should be able to fill two jars). cover them with the salted vinegar, leaving a little room at the top but making sure peppers are completely covered. Gently tap the jars on the counter to remove any air bubbles. Top off the jars with extra-virgin olive oil. Store in the fridge.

Notes

Vegan Parmesan Cheese Dust

Servings: 8
Time: 10 minutes

- ¼ cup sunflower seeds (roasted, salted)
- ¾ cup cashews (raw)
- ⅓ cup nutritional yeast
- 1 tsp garlic powder
- 1 tsp onion powder
- ½ tsp sea salt

How it's made

1. Place everything in a food chopper or food processor and blend until it's a fine powder.

Notes

This Is Just The Beginning

At the end of the day, if we just become more aware of the "what" is in our food, we have power. We control the direction of our health. It's not about weird diets or labeling how we eat. You don't have to become vegan (and if you choose to be vegan, that is awesome too), or starve yourself. It's definitely not healthy to do a low-fat diet, and you don't need to count every carb and calorie.

If this book teaches you anything I hope that it's this:

- Try to lower the inflammatory foods in your diet: foods like dairy, gluten, white refined sugar, overly processed foods, and takeout.

- Begin to read your food labels. Stop putting all your focus on the nutrition facts and begin reading the ingredient list. When I was attending school, one thing they taught us was "The ingredient list tells you the whole story of the food. And if you choose foods with good ingredient lists, the nutrition facts will take care of themselves," meaning that if the ingredient list is full of healthy ingredients, your nutrition will follow.

- Spend a little more time at the grocery store. Don't be in a hurry when choosing your food. Push your cart out of the way of others so you can read those food labels.

- Buy high-quality meats, poultry, and seafood. Organic, grass-fed, and wild caught are the way to go.

- Stop buying refined oils and throw out foods in your pantry that contain these oils.

- Drink more water. That, in itself, can heal and be one of the most powerful tools your body needs.

- Spend a little more time in your kitchen. Afterall, that is where your health begins. Celebrate your health by creating healthier recipes.

This journey is just beginning for me. There are big things coming and I can feel it in my soul. I am passionate and I am determined to make a huge difference in the way people think about and treat food. When I empower others to take the reins on their health by changing their food patterns, it lights a bigger fire under me to keep going, keep learning, and keep inspiring.

Remember this: It's in the little decisions. Your health depends on what you choose to eat every single day. Food is the tool for optimal health. It starts in the kitchen...not the doctor's office.

I'm grateful for you. I'm rooting for you. And I'm always behind you whispering, "You too can do this."

Xoxo

Acknowledgements

I could not have taken the time to create these recipes and write this book if it weren't for my best friend and husband, Neil. Neil has supported me from the day I said I wanted to attend nutrition school. He has been my guinea pig, my science project, my listening ear, and even taken some food pictures for me. Through all my crazy ideas and the chasing of dreams, he stands by me. I know not everyone has a "Neil" in their life, but I do. I'm so grateful for him. Thank you, Neil, for being by my side every single day. I love you.

And to my parents and my two boys Sterling & Stiles, thank you! You are such a supportive family that I'm eternally grateful for. Mom, you always say you are a cheerleader in my life. You've always been in the wings, behind the scenes, supporting my endeavors. To my boys... how did I get so lucky to be your mom?? You really are the coolest humans. You always send me encouraging words, reply to my silly social media posts and tell me how proud you are of me. Dad, thanks for always sharing my social posts and (sometimes) trying my recipes. We call ourselves the Fam Damily and I'll never give up on the mission to get you to eat healthier. Ever.

Thank you, Neil, Mom, Dad, Sterling, and Stiles. I love you. And I have one thing to say...eat more greens!

PS: Thank you Jenny Martell – **@jmar_portraits** – for taking such wonderful pictures of me for this project. You really took me out of my comfort zone and let my personality shine through these photos.

Index